THE ATLANTA AND SAVANNAH CAMPAIGNS

1864

by
J. Britt McCarley

Center of Military History
United States Army
Washington, D.C., 2014

INTRODUCTION

Although over one hundred fifty years have passed since the start of the American Civil War, that titanic conflict continues to matter. The forces unleashed by that war were immensely destructive because of the significant issues involved: the existence of the Union, the end of slavery, and the very future of the nation. The war remains our most contentious, and our bloodiest, with over six hundred thousand killed in the course of the four-year struggle.

Most civil wars do not spring up overnight, and the American Civil War was no exception. The seeds of the conflict were sown in the earliest days of the republic's founding, primarily over the existence of slavery and the slave trade. Although no conflict can begin without the conscious decisions of those engaged in the debates at that moment, in the end, there was simply no way to paper over the division of the country into two camps: one that was dominated by slavery and the other that sought first to limit its spread and then to abolish it. Our nation was indeed "half slave and half free," and that could not stand.

Regardless of the factors tearing the nation asunder, the soldiers on each side of the struggle went to war for personal reasons: looking for adventure, being caught up in the passions and emotions of their peers, believing in the Union, favoring states' rights, or even justifying the simple schoolyard dynamic of being convinced that they were "worth" three of the soldiers on the other side. Nor can we overlook the factor that some went to war to prove their manhood. This has been, and continues to be, a key dynamic in understanding combat and the profession of arms. Soldiers join for many reasons but often stay in the fight because of their comrades and because they do not want to seem like cowards. Sometimes issues of national impact shrink to nothing in the intensely personal world of cannon shell and minié ball.

Whatever the reasons, the struggle was long and costly and only culminated with the conquest of the rebellious Confederacy, the preservation of the Union, and the end of slavery. These campaign pamphlets on the American Civil War, prepared in commemoration of our national sacrifices, seek to remember that war and honor those in the United States Army who died to preserve the Union and free the slaves as well as to tell the story of those American soldiers who fought for the Confederacy despite the inherently flawed nature of their cause. The Civil War was our greatest struggle and continues to deserve our deep study and contemplation.

RICHARD W. STEWART, PH.D.
Chief of Military History

THE ATLANTA AND SAVANNAH CAMPAIGNS
1864

Strategic Setting

In 1864, as the Civil War entered its fourth year, the most devastating conflict in American history seemed to grind on with no end in sight. In order to break the stalemate, President Abraham Lincoln appointed Maj. Gen. Ulysses S. Grant general in chief of the U.S. Army and nominated him for promotion to lieutenant general, which Congress duly confirmed on 2 March. As the North's most successful field commander, Grant had built his reputation in the Western Theater, which stretched from the Appalachian Mountains in the east to the Mississippi River in the west and from the Ohio River in the north to the Gulf of Mexico in the south. His impressive résumé included victories at Forts Henry and Donelson, Tennessee; Shiloh, Tennessee; Vicksburg, Mississippi; and Chattanooga, Tennessee. Before heading east to assume his new duties, Grant designated his most trusted subordinate, Maj. Gen. William T. Sherman, to succeed him as commander of the Military Division of the Mississippi, a sprawling geographic command that spanned most of the Western Theater.

Sherman traveled with Grant as far as Cincinnati, Ohio. During the trip, the two men devised the Union Army's grand strategy. In the coming campaigns, all Federal forces would advance as one; the main effort would occur on two fronts. Grant would attack General Robert E. Lee's Army of Northern Virginia, which defended Richmond, the Confederate capital. Sherman's objective was General Joseph E. Johnston's Army of Tennessee, which

General Sherman
(Library of Congress)

protected Atlanta, Georgia, the largest manufacturing and transportation center in the Deep South. Grant directed Sherman "to move against Johnston's army, to break it up, and to get into the interior of the enemy's country as far as you can, inflicting all the damage you can against their war resources." Through unified action, the Federals would prevent the two main Confederate armies from reinforcing each other, as they had done in 1863.

After meeting with Grant, Sherman headed to Nashville, Tennessee, and assumed command of the three armies he would lead in the Atlanta Campaign. By far the largest was Maj. Gen. George H. Thomas' 75,000-strong Army of the Cumberland, consisting of Maj. Gen. Oliver O. Howard's IV Corps, Maj. Gen. John M. Palmer's XIV Corps, Maj. Gen. Joseph Hooker's XX Corps, and Brig. Gen. Washington L. Elliott's cavalry corps. Next in size was Sherman's former command, the 25,000-man Army of the Tennessee led by Maj. Gen. James B. McPherson, which comprised Maj. Gen. John A. "Black Jack" Logan's XV Corps and two small divisions from the XVI Corps under Brig. Gen. Grenville M. Dodge. The third and smallest was Maj. Gen. John M. Schofield's 13,000-strong Army of the Ohio, composed of the XXIII Corps and Maj. Gen. George Stoneman's cavalry division. In addition to the infantry and cavalry units, Sherman's army group boasted an artillery component numbering 254 guns commanded by Brig. Gen. William F. Barry. Altogether, Sherman led over 113,000 tough and confident soldiers who had known mostly success against their Confederate adversaries in the West.

A vast array of depots, warehouses, and arsenals linked by an extensive railroad network supported Sherman's army group. The logistical chain began at Louisville, Kentucky, Sherman's base of operations; continued south to the forward base at Nashville; and ended at Chattanooga, the advanced depot. The two most important railroads were the Louisville and Nashville and the Nashville and Chattanooga, both private lines that functioned under the Army's U.S. Military Railroad agency. South of Nashville, railroad guards, regular troop detachments, and combined arms expeditions operating in Tennessee, Alabama, and Mississippi provided security against Confederate guerrillas and cavalry raiders bent on cutting Sherman's supply line. In 1864, the Military Division of the Mississippi operated from 744 to 1,062 miles of railroad. During the buildup for the Atlanta Campaign, an average of 145 railcars arrived at Chattanooga each day carrying 1,600 tons of supplies, including ammunition, provisions for soldiers and animals, uniforms, weapons, and equipment, until the army's warehouses fairly burst at the seams by early May.

Federal rail operations extended nearly to the fighting front throughout the march to Atlanta, with 5,000 Army wagons pulled by 33,000 mules carrying supplies from the railhead to the combat troops. Over 28,000 horses kept officers and cavalrymen mounted or served as draft animals for the artillery batteries. In addition, 900 horse-drawn ambulances transported battlefield casualties. Georgia's state-owned Western and Atlantic Railroad connected Atlanta, the Gate City of the South, with Chattanooga, a distance of 140 rail miles. Both the Northern and the Southern armies used the Western and Atlantic—the Federal rail line running south from Chattanooga and the Confederate line heading north from Atlanta.

Opposing Sherman's legions was the Army of Tennessee under General Johnston. One of the ranking officers in the antebellum Regular Army, Johnston had risen to quartermaster general before resigning his commission and offering his services to the Confederacy. He was quickly appointed as a full general in the Confederate Army. He commanded the main Confederate army in the field in Virginia until he was wounded at the Battle of Seven Pines in the spring of 1862, losing his command to Robert E. Lee in June of that year. During his tenure, he had often quarreled with Confederate President Jefferson Davis, establishing a contentious relationship that worsened over time. In December 1863, Davis had appointed Johnston commander of the Army of Tennessee only after his first choice, Lt. Gen. William J. Hardee, had refused the job. Further aggravating an already tense situation was a memorandum that Johnston had submitted to Davis in January

General Johnston
(National Archives)

General Hardee
(Library of Congress)

1864 proposing that slaves be recruited and armed as soldiers. The proposal was the brainchild of Maj. Gen. Patrick R. Cleburne, one of Johnston's division commanders. The Confederate president had found the document so inflammatory that he immediately suppressed it.

At the start of the Atlanta Campaign, the Army of Tennessee numbered about 55,000 men divided into three corps. Since its inception, the Confederacy's second-largest field army had suffered one defeat after another before it achieved a stunning victory at Chickamauga, Georgia, in September 1863, only to be routed at Chattanooga just two months later. Commanding the two infantry corps were General Hardee and Lt. Gen. John B. Hood, and Maj. Gen. Joseph Wheeler led the cavalry corps. The artillery consisted of 144 guns and was commanded by Brig. Gen. Francis A. Shoup. In short, the Confederates in northern Georgia were outnumbered by roughly two to one. In mid-May, President Davis improved the odds considerably by transferring Lt. Gen. Leonidas Polk's Army of Mississippi to the Army of Tennessee, providing an additional 20,000 troops for the defense of Atlanta.

Unlike the Federals, the Confederates had devised no overarching campaign plan. Shortly before Johnston had assumed command of the army, Davis had written him a long letter painting a rosy picture of the army's condition, conveying the "hope that you will soon be able to commence active operations against the enemy," defeat the Federal force at Chattanooga, and recapture lost territory in Tennessee. The ever-cautious Johnston replied that "difficulties appear to me [to be] in the way" of assuming an aggressive posture. He maintained that "I can see no other mode of taking the offensive here than to beat the enemy when he advances, and then move forward. But to make victory probable, the army must be strengthened." Johnston offered numerous reasons for remaining on the defensive, ranging from logistical difficulties to the enemy's superior numbers. This exchange set the pattern for future correspondence between Davis and Johnston, in which the president would attempt to prod the general into attacking, only to be told that the conditions for an assault were unfavorable.

After the Federals had driven the Confederates from the mountain ridges overlooking Chattanooga, the Army of Tennessee established its winter camp at Dalton, Georgia. Johnston anchored his defensive line on Rocky Face Ridge, which rose 700 feet above the surrounding plain and extended 15 miles south to the north bank of the Oostanaula River beyond Resaca, Georgia. An army could cross the rugged ridgeline at only three points: Mill Creek Gap—also known as Buzzard Roost—northwest of Dalton and through which the Western and Atlantic Railroad passed; man-made Dug Gap, southwest of Dalton; and the tortuous Snake Creek Gap, northwest of Resaca. Despite its menacing appearance, Rocky Face Ridge had several weaknesses. First, the northern end was open to attack from Cleveland, Tennessee. Second, the railroad ran along the eastern face, leaving it vulnerable to interdiction from the three gaps. Third, Rocky Face's seeming natural strength, especially along its northern end, fed Johnston's careless hope that Sherman would oblige him by launching frontal assaults against his positions (*Map 1*).

In reality, Sherman's plan for dealing with the Confederate stronghold at Dalton evolved over time, assuming final form only after he had responded to changing conditions. He initially considered having Thomas and Schofield demonstrate against Rocky Face, while McPherson executed a deep turning movement from his northeastern Alabama base to threaten the industrial center of Rome, Georgia, about fifty miles southwest of Dalton. But Johnston had anticipated Sherman's operational plan and sent Polk's command to defend Rome.

What Johnston had failed to foresee was an attack on Resaca via Snake Creek Gap. Though aware of the gap and the danger it

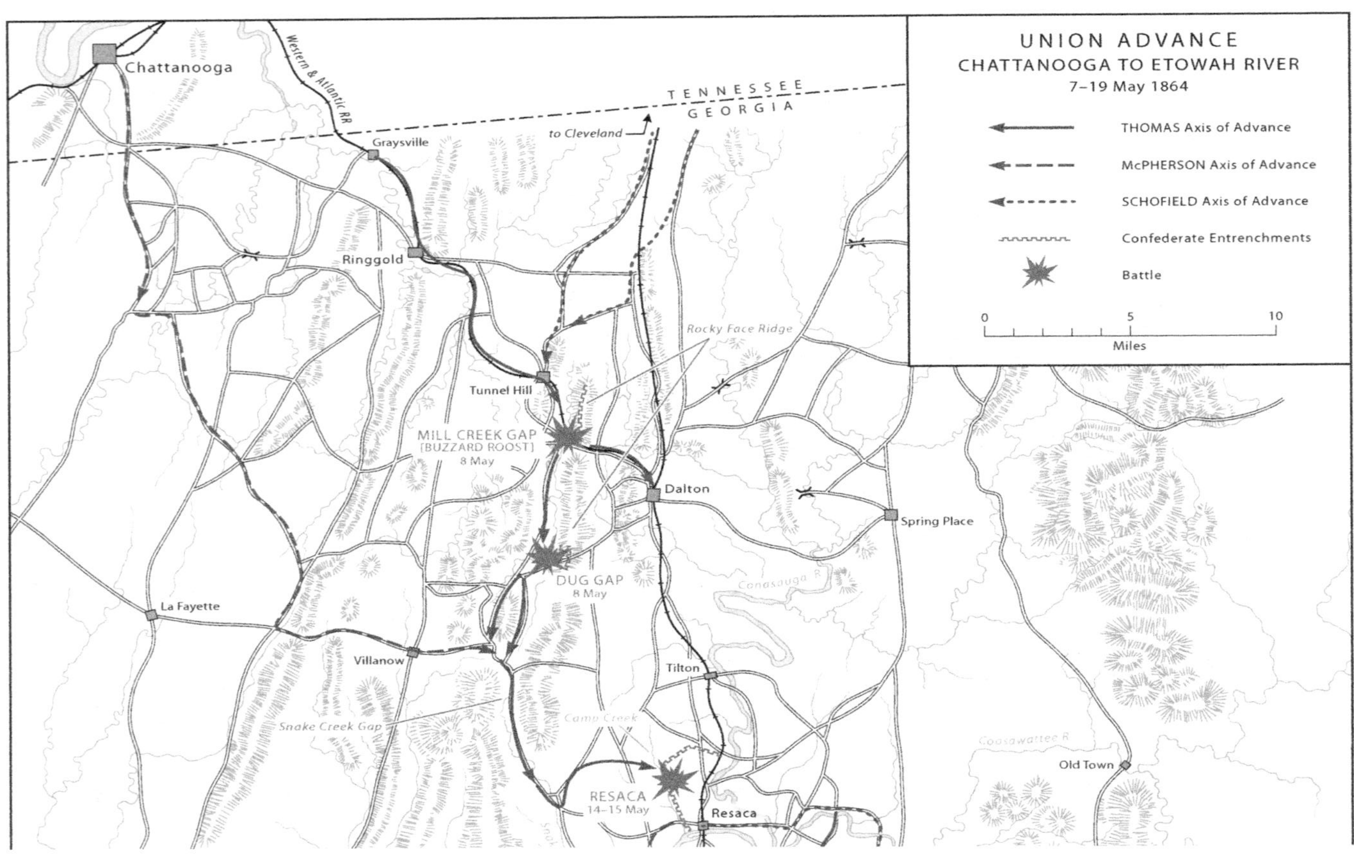

UNION ADVANCE
CHATTANOOGA TO ETOWAH RIVER
7–19 May 1864
THOMAS Axis of Advance
McPHERSON Axis of Advance
SCHOFIELD Axis of Advance
Confederate Entrenchments
Battle
0
5
10
Miles
Chattanooga
Western & Atlantic RR
TENNESSEE
GEORGIA
to Cleveland
Graysville
Ringgold
Tunnel Hill
Rocky Face Ridge
MILL CREEK GAP
[BUZZARD ROOST]
8 May
Dalton
Spring Place
DUG GAP
8 May
Conasauga R
La Fayette
Villanow
Tilton
Snake Creek Gap
Camp Creek
Coosawattee R
Old Town
RESACA
14–15 May
Resaca

Adamsville
Summerville
LAY'S FERRY
15–16 May
Calhoun
Adairsville
Gravelly Plateau
Hermitage
Oostanaula R.
Rome
Coosaville
Kingston
CASSVILLE
19 May
Cass Station
Etowah R.
Coosa R.
Western & Atlantic RR
Euharlee
Allatoona
Etowah R.

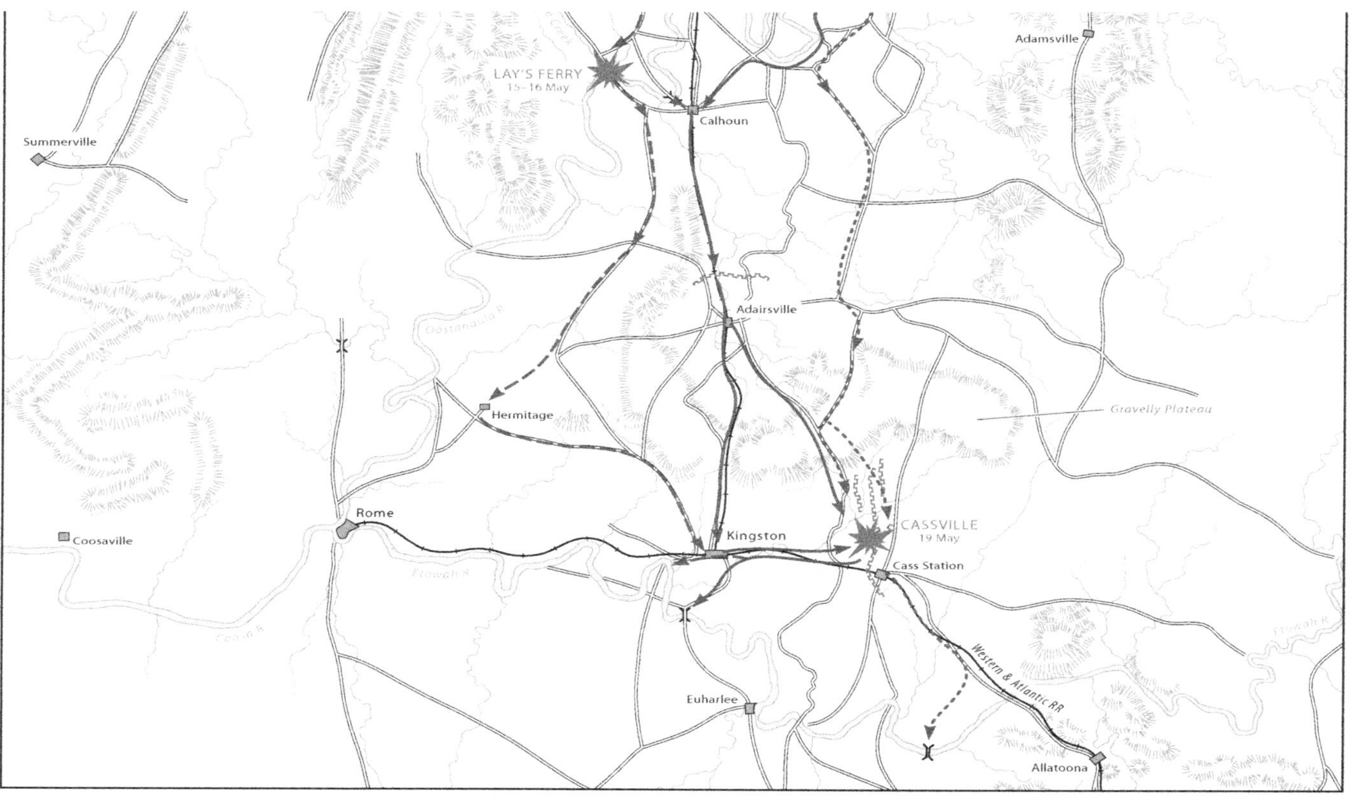

MAP 1

posed to his line of communications, he had failed to post a cavalry detachment in a position to detect enemy movements there. While Sherman knew nothing about this critical omission, he soon benefited from it. Due to detachments resulting from bureaucratic miscues and Maj. Gen. Nathaniel P. Banks' Red River campaign in Louisiana, McPherson's army was left with only four of its nine divisions, rendering an advance on Rome impractical. Instead, Sherman decided to send McPherson through Snake Creek Gap to cut the Western and Atlantic at Resaca. To the north but within supporting distance, Thomas would conduct diversionary attacks along Rocky Face Ridge from Mill Creek Gap to Dug Gap, while Schofield threatened Dalton from the north. Sherman's intent was to pry Johnston's army from its entrenchments by placing McPherson's army on the railroad between the Confederates and Atlanta. Johnston would be forced to fight in the open to regain his supply line, presenting Sherman with an opportunity to destroy the Army of Tennessee in one decisive battle at the start of the campaign.

Operations

From Rocky Face Ridge to Resaca

The Atlanta Campaign began on 7 May 1864, when the Union IV, XIV, and XXIII Corps advanced toward Rocky Face Ridge at Mill Creek Gap and into Crow Valley north of Dalton to distract the Confederates. On the next day, the XX Corps attacked at Dug Gap in a further effort to divert Johnston's attention. In the meantime, lead elements of McPherson's army reached the unguarded western entrance to Snake Creek Gap after scrambling over undulating terrain characteristic of northwestern Georgia. Johnston remained oblivious to the threat to Resaca—focusing instead on Dalton to the north and Rome to the southwest—while Wheeler's cavalry monitored every approach to the south except Snake Creek Gap. Concern for the safety of Rome led Johnston to spread Polk's force from there to Resaca. On 7 May, units of Brig. Gen. James Cantey's division arrived at Resaca and began digging in along the hills west of the railroad bridge over the Oostanaula, their position overlooking Camp Creek.

About 1600 on 9 May, McPherson's troops first encountered Southern cavalry between Snake Creek Gap and Cantey's earthworks. McPherson's mission was to cut the Western and Atlantic at Resaca and then head north, attacking Johnston's army as it withdrew south from Dalton. But the discovery of Confederates where he had expected none caused McPherson to lose sight of his objective. He halted, evaluated the situation, and decided to withdraw to the gap, fearing that a lack of cavalry would leave him vulnerable as he advanced north toward Johnston's army. Sherman later chided McPherson for his loss of nerve: "Well, Mac, you have missed the opportunity of a lifetime."

General McPherson
(Library of Congress)

To his credit, Johnston responded quickly and effectively to the sudden threat at Snake Creek Gap. First, he sent Hood's three divisions south toward Resaca. Then, from 10 to 12 May, he halted all of Polk's arriving units at Resaca and placed Polk in command there. When Wheeler's troopers reported that nearly all of Sherman's units had left Dalton, Johnston immediately ordered his remaining infantry to march to Resaca. The Confederate chieftain correctly guessed that Sherman intended to cut off the Army of Tennessee from its supply line and then destroy it. By 12 May, most of Sherman's army group had crowded into the Snake Creek Gap area to strike Resaca. Howard's IV Corps was the sole exception, marching along the Western and Atlantic Railroad from Dalton toward Resaca, its progress slowed by Wheeler's cavalry.

By 14 May, most Confederate and Federal units had arrived at Resaca. The Southerners held the high ground east of Camp Creek and west of the Western and Atlantic. Polk's command, now functioning as a corps under Johnston's direction, anchored the Confederate left resting on the Oostanaula downstream from the railroad bridge. Hardee's corps occupied the center of the Confederate line, with Hood's corps holding the right and extending to the Conasauga River, which joined the Coosawattee River nearby to form the Oostanaula. The right-angle junction between Hardee's right and Hood's left resulted in a salient on high ground held by two infantry brigades and three artillery batteries. Wheeler's cavalry covered the Confederate right beyond the Conasauga, while Brig. Gen. William H. Jackson's cavalry division of Polk's corps and one of Hardee's infantry divisions protected the left flank across the Oostanaula.

Despite these preparations, the Confederates occupied a potentially dangerous position, with the bulk of their forces hemmed in by a river on each flank and by a third stream behind them. On the opposite side of Camp Creek, McPherson's army occupied the right of the Union line, reaching to the Oostanaula. On McPherson's left, Hooker's XX Corps and Palmer's XIV Corps extended the Federal line, followed by Schofield's XXIII Corps, which nevertheless ended far short of the Conasauga. Not until early on the first day of battle at Resaca did Howard's IV Corps deploy on the Union left flank, but the line still failed to reach the Conasauga, making it vulnerable to an attack.

Flaws in his deployments notwithstanding, Sherman's first-day battle plan called for his army group to hit Confederate positions vigorously enough to prevent Johnston from shifting units to confront Brig. Gen. Thomas W. Sweeny's XVI Corps division as it crossed the Oostanaula downstream from Resaca. Once across, Sweeny's men would march east to cut the Western and Atlantic at Calhoun, Georgia, in the Confederate rear.

The Union diversionary assault began about 1300 on 14 May. Consisting of a division each from the XIV and the XXIII Corps, the Federal attackers slogged across the miry bottomlands along Camp Creek in order to strike the enemy salient. The Confederate defenders repulsed the onslaught with blasts of double-shotted canister—a lethal antipersonnel round—fired by several Southern batteries. From its vantage point east of the Conasauga, Wheeler's cavalry reported the Federal left flank open to attack, and Johnston rushed units from the Confederate left to reinforce Hood's right. At roughly 1600, Hood struck with the divisions of Maj. Gens. Carter L. Stevenson and Alexander P. Stewart, and they routed the slow-moving IV Corps before it could entrench. A lone Indiana battery firing double-shotted canister and the timely arrival of Brig. Gen. Alpheus S. Williams' XX Corps division were all that kept Sherman's left flank from being overwhelmed. Pleased with the day's results, Johnston directed Hood to renew the attack early the next morning.

To the south, elements of the Union XV Corps west of Camp Creek seized a hill that placed the Western and Atlantic Railroad bridge within easy reach of Federal artillery, and they established a lodgment on the east bank of the creek. These Union successes forced Johnston to lay a pontoon bridge farther up the Oostanaula to remain connected with the railroad and the defenders south of Resaca. Having weakened his left to support Hood's attacks, Johnston lacked the means to drive off the XV Corps.

At first, Sweeny's crossing operation at Lay's Ferry on the Oostanaula—near the point where Snake Creek flows into the river—proceeded according to plan, with Union troops crossing on pontoon boats and scattering Confederate cavalrymen as they reached the opposite bank. Then the operation began to unravel. For the rest of the day and well into the night, uncertainty reigned on both sides regarding the situation at Lay's Ferry. Had the Federals crossed there, and, if so, had the rebels attempted to dislodge them? Crediting unsubstantiated intelligence that the enemy had crossed the river and now threatened his position, Sweeny withdrew to the north bank of the Oostanaula. Due to confusing reports about Sweeny's presence at Lay's Ferry, Johnston decided to cancel Hood's dawn attack. That night, Sherman sent Hooker's two remaining divisions to the Union left and directed Sweeny to recross the Oostanaula the next morning.

Starting about 1130 on 15 May, Hood repelled several attacks launched by the IV and the XX Corps. But the 70th Indiana Infantry under Col. Benjamin Harrison managed to seize a Confederate redoubt that occupied a critical point in front of Hood's main line. In doing so, the Hoosiers captured the four cannons of Capt. Maximilian van den Corput's Cherokee Georgia Battery, but enemy fire prevented the Federals from removing the guns. That night, Brig. Gen. John W. Geary, a XX Corps division commander, sent the 5th Ohio Infantry out to retrieve the guns. Assisted by several other troop detachments, the Buckeyes drew off the cannons. The incident was highly publicized and later helped to elect Colonel Harrison president of the United States in 1888.

Johnston's plan for 15 May remained virtually the same as it had been the day before: Hardee was to reinforce Hood for another assault on the Union left near the Conasauga. Continuing uncertainty over Federal operations at Lay's Ferry had led Johnston to cancel the attack order and then postpone the assault until late afternoon, only to cancel it yet again—but not before Hood struck the Union left flank at 1600 and was repulsed with heavy losses. Meanwhile, Sweeny's division recrossed the Oostanaula at Lay's Ferry. Using an abandoned flatboat, the Federals secured a lodgment on the south bank, enabling engineers to lay a pontoon bridge there. Sweeny's presence at the ferry threatened Johnston's Western and Atlantic supply line, rendering his position at Resaca untenable. The Army of Tennessee evacuated its fortifications at night and began marching south toward Calhoun.

Thus ended the two-day Battle of Resaca—the first major engagement of the Atlanta Campaign. Northern losses totaled roughly 4,000, while Southern casualties came to about 3,000. Although the Confederates had launched several assaults against the Federal line, Sherman had retained the initiative throughout the operation. By sending Sweeny's division to seize Lay's Ferry, he maneuvered Johnston out of an apparently strong position at Resaca. Sherman thereby established an operational pattern he would use throughout the campaign. Using the bulk of his army group to fix Johnston's army in place, Sherman would send a flying column to sever the Confederate supply line, forcing Johnston to choose between fighting a battle in the open or withdrawing to the next strongpoint on the road to Atlanta.

Cassville and the Dallas–New Hope Church–Pickett's Mill Line

The region that the armies now entered was generally flatter and more arable than the rugged terrain through which they had just passed. The remainder of Polk's corps arrived, raising the Army of Tennessee's troop strength to 70,000. Johnston intended to fall back along the Western and Atlantic Railroad, occupying a succession of blocking positions while tempting Sherman into launching a potentially disastrous frontal assault. Because he had failed to make a careful study of the topography south of Dalton, Johnston discovered few naturally strong positions on which to anchor a defensive line. As a result, he withdrew from both Calhoun and Adairsville, Georgia, during 16 to 18 May, his rear guard delaying the Union pursuit. As the Federals passed through Adairsville, Sherman decided to split his army group into three segments to quicken the pace. While one of McPherson's divisions followed the Oostanaula River southwest to Rome, the rest of the Army of the Tennessee, followed by Thomas' IV and XIV Corps, took the road south from Adairsville toward Kingston, Georgia. Only Hooker's XX Corps and

Schofield's XXIII Corps took the southeasterly road to Cassville, Georgia, a declining town that the railroad had bypassed years before. With the Federals thus divided, Johnston decided to spring a trap on the Union column marching toward Cassville.

Johnston prepared his ambush with care. He first sent Hardee's corps and the army's wagon train to the south to assume a blocking position on the Kingston Road. Then he directed Polk's corps to deploy along Two Run Creek north of Cassville and block the Adairsville Road. Hood would form on Polk's right and occupy a range of hills overlooking the road. Polk and Hood were to attack the approaching Union column and destroy it. On the morning of 19 May, Johnston took his place with the ambush force, having just issued a blustering order: "Soldiers of the Army of Tennessee . . . I lead you to battle." But the commanding general's confidence soon gave way to doubt, as Hood reported a Union force of unknown strength advancing on his rear from the east. Losing his nerve, Johnston ordered Hood and Polk to withdraw south of Cassville. He later regretted his decision. Though small, the Union column was no phantom, and yet Johnston believed that Hood had overreacted. Up to this point, Johnston had regarded Hood as a protégé, but the incident at Cassville shook his confidence in the younger man. To make matters worse, the budding Johnston-Hood command partnership had generated considerable resentment among Hardee and other subordinates, further poisoning the atmosphere at army headquarters.

In any event, a Confederate assault at Cassville might well have failed anyway because it was unlikely that Hood and Polk together could have defeated both Schofield and Hooker. Moreover, Thomas had approached to within supporting distance by midmorning of 19 May. Worse yet, Union artillery fire from the hills north of town soon rendered Johnston's line untenable. That night, after conferring with several of his senior commanders, Johnston ordered a withdrawal to the Etowah River. The Army of Tennessee retreated yet again, the foot soldiers' pace quickening in response to news that Federal cavalry had seized a bridge over the Etowah southwest of Cassville. Johnston's pattern of retreating in order to avoid battle played into Sherman's hands, enabling him to cover half the distance from Dalton to Atlanta in barely two weeks. As a result, Union morale soared while Confederate morale began to sink. But the return to hillier, more defensible terrain seemed to indicate more fighting ahead.

The terrain south of the Etowah River was rugged and heavily forested with few roads. Johnston initially posted his army in the Allatoona Mountains south of the river, near the Western and Atlantic Railroad cut known as the Allatoona Pass. Recalling the terrain from a journey he had made there in the 1840s, Sherman decided to cross the Etowah more to the west, where the hills lay farther south from the river and the countryside was flatter. Aiming for the town of Dallas, Georgia, about fifteen miles south of the river, Sherman intended to outflank Johnston from the Allatoona Mountains all the way back to the Chattahoochee River, about ten miles northwest of Atlanta. (*See Map 2.*)

Sherman gave his armies a few days' rest before setting out for Dallas. For the first time in the campaign, the Federals were operating away from their railroad lifeline and having to carry their supplies. On 23 May, they crossed the Etowah with twenty days' rations stuffed into their knapsacks, haversacks, and supply wagons. McPherson marched on the right, Thomas in the center, and Schofield on the left, gradually changing direction from south to east. True to character, Sherman fretted ceaselessly along the way. "We are now all in motion like a vast hive of bees," he wrote, "and expect to swarm along the Chattahoochee in five days." His timetable proved overoptimistic, for it would take him six weeks rather than five days to reach the Chattahoochee and the outskirts of Atlanta.

When Confederate cavalry reported the renewed Federal advance, Johnston left Hood to guard Allatoona Pass, sent Hardee toward Dallas, and placed Polk between the two. After a single day's hard march, Sherman's men neared the town from several directions. Realizing that the Dallas crossroads was Sherman's objective, Johnston concentrated his army there on 24 May. Hardee held the Confederate left, followed by Polk in the center and Hood on the right. From their vantage point on the crest of Elsberry Mountain, the rebels observed the approaching Union forces to the west.

On 25 May, the Federals crossed Pumpkin Vine Creek west of Dallas, heading east. Johnston directed Hood to occupy the crossroads at New Hope Church, about four miles to the northeast. By midmorning, Hood's three divisions had deployed around the Methodist log meetinghouse, with Maj. Gen. Thomas C. Hindman's division on the left, Stewart's division in the center, and Stevenson's division on the right. Hardee and Polk formed on Hood's left. Union prisoners reported Hooker's XX Corps nearby. Indeed,

Geary's division was heading straight for the church, accompanied by Thomas and Hooker. Confederate prisoners indicated that a large enemy force lay ahead. In response, Geary dug in, Hooker summoned his two remaining divisions, and Thomas alerted two more Union corps. Sherman also happened to be in the area, and he incorrectly assumed that Hooker was on Johnston's right flank. The sparse roads, rugged terrain, and dense woods contributed to the Federals' confusion about the enemy's location and strength.

Meanwhile, the skies darkened, and rain began to fall, heralding a month of foul weather that would drastically alter the campaign's tempo. Torrential rains soon transformed the roads into quagmires, making them virtually impassable. The weather turned hot and humid, and swarms of mosquitoes and other insects plagued the men incessantly. Dwindling supplies only added to their misery. Small wonder the soldiers in blue nick-named the region around Dallas "the Hell Hole."

The XX Corps began its movement about 1600, struggling through tangled thickets toward the crossroads, with Maj. Gen. Daniel A. Butterfield's division on the left, Geary in the center, and Williams on the right, each division compressed into a narrow column. The battle developed into a clash between Williams' Union division and Stewart's Confederate division, the latter protected by log breastworks and supported by sixteen cannons. It was no contest. As the weather deteriorated, Williams suffered about 800 casualties, while Geary and Butterfield lost another 800 men combined. Confederate losses came to about 350 troops. Sherman blamed Hooker for the XX Corps' failure to seize the crossroads, which the latter bitterly resented.

On the following day, 26 May, McPherson held Dallas, Thomas confronted New Hope Church, and Schofield extended the Federal left toward Pickett's Mill. Union cavalry secured both flanks, but a gap separated McPherson and Thomas. Johnston's three corps continued to occupy the same positions, except that Cleburne's division of Hardee's corps now extended the Confederate right beyond Hood's position toward Pickett's Mill. Confederate cavalry covered both flanks.

On 27 May, Sherman attempted to turn the strengthened Southern right flank. More than just a flanking maneuver, it was also part of a gradual shift back to the Western and Atlantic. Sherman's army group had so few supply wagons that it could not operate far from the railroad for long. Although the Federals

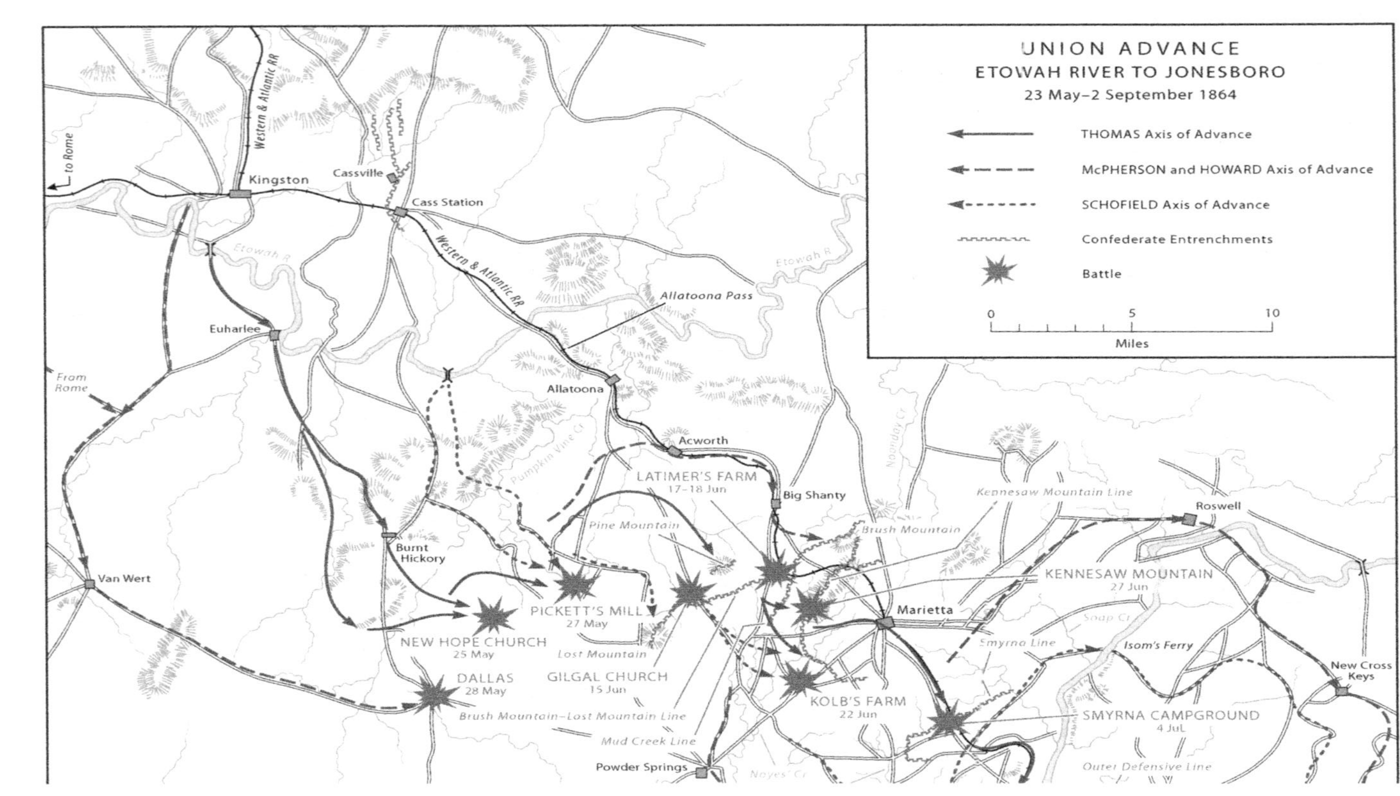

UNION ADVANCE
ETOWAH RIVER TO JONESBORO
23 May–2 September 1864
THOMAS Axis of Advance
McPHERSON and HOWARD Axis of Advance
SCHOFIELD Axis of Advance
Confederate Entrenchments
Battle
0
5
10
Miles
to Rome
Kingston
Cassville
Cass Station
Western & Atlantic RR
Western & Atlantic RR
Etowah R.
Etowah R.
Euharlee
Allatoona Pass
Allatoona
Acworth
Van Wert
From Rome
Burnt Hickory
LATIMER'S FARM
17–18 Jun
Big Shanty
Pumpkin Vine Cr.
Pine Mountain
Lost Mountain
NEW HOPE CHURCH
25 May
PICKETT'S MILL
27 May
DALLAS
28 May
GILGAL CHURCH
15 Jun
Brush Mountain–Lost Mountain Line
Mud Creek Line
Powder Springs
Brush Mountain
Kennesaw Mountain Line
KENNESAW MOUNTAIN
27 Jun
Marietta
KOLB'S FARM
22 Jun
Noonday Cr.
Noyes Cr.
Snap Cr.
Smyrna Line
Isom's Ferry
SMYRNA CAMPGROUND
4 Jul
Outer Defensive Line
Roswell
New Cross Keys

Buckhead
PEACHTREE CREEK
20 Jul
Georgia RR
Sweet Water
Mason and Turner's Ferry
Chattahoochee River Line
Atlanta
Decatur
ATLANTA
22 Jul
Sandtown
Utoy
EZRA CHURCH
28 Jul
Fortifications of Atlanta
UTOY CREEK
6 Aug
East Point
Railroad Defense Line
Campbellton
Rough and Ready
Red Oak
Macon & Western RR
Fairburn
Atlanta & West Pont RR
County Line
JONESBORO
31 Aug–1 Sep
Jonesboro
Palmetto
Jonesboro Line
Fayetteville
Flint R.
Fosterville
Lovejoy Station Line
Lovejoy's Station

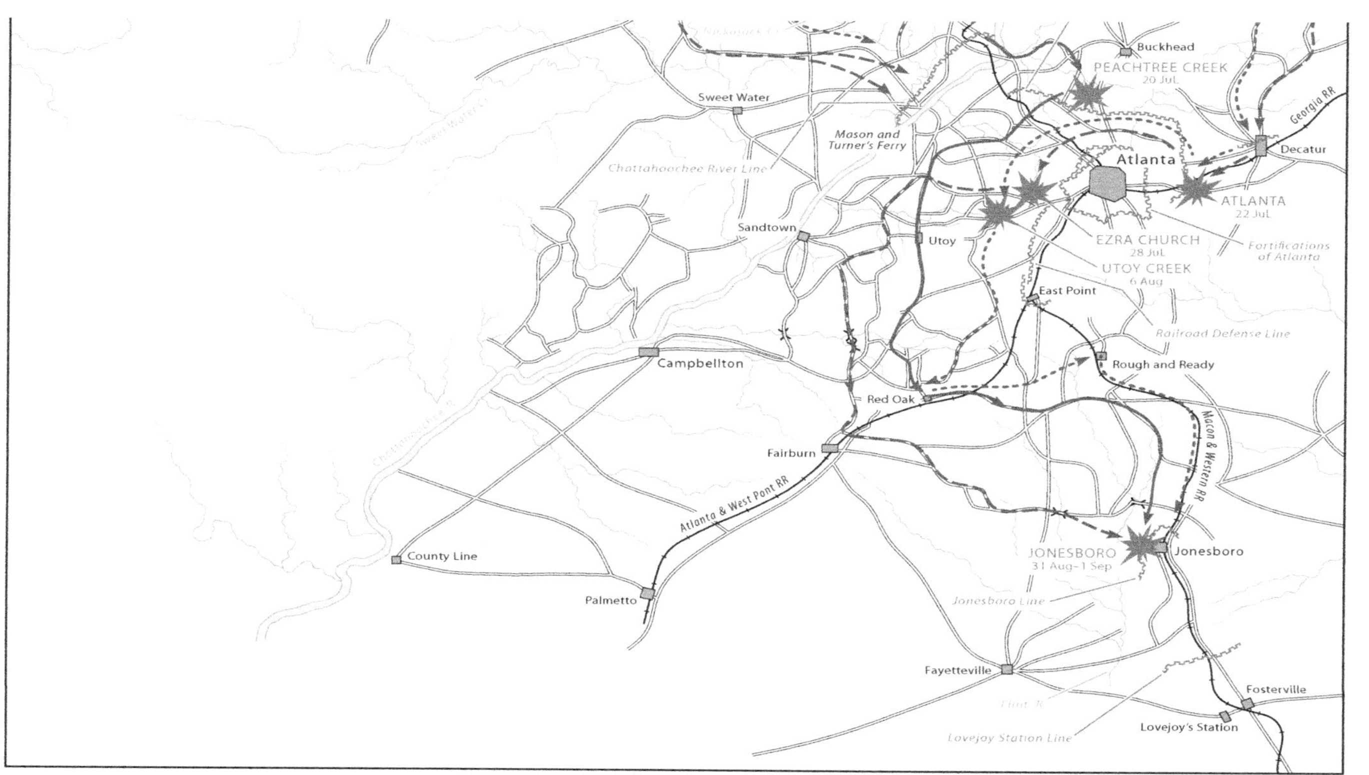

MAP 2

had started with twenty days' rations, they had already consumed most of their provisions. Sherman started the flanking maneuver by ordering Howard to assemble a task force from the XIV Corps, the XXIII Corps, and his own IV Corps. He then directed Howard to turn Johnston's right flank near Pickett's Mill and strike the Confederate rear area. In the meantime, units along the rest of the Federal line were to divert the Southerners' attention.

About 1100, Howard's task force began its flank march and was soon discovered by Confederate scouts. Along the way, Howard became disoriented and sent word to Thomas: "No person can appreciate the difficulty in moving over this ground unless he can see it," Howard wrote. "I am . . . facing south, and am now turning the enemy's right flank, I think." Howard was mistaken, however. On reaching the jump-off point for the attack, he gave his troops a breather and then deployed them. He formed Brig. Gen. Thomas J. Wood's IV Corps division in the center in column of brigades, while posting Brig. Gen. Richard W. Johnson's XIV Corps division on the left and Brig. Gen. Nathaniel C. McLean's XXIII Corps brigade on the right for support. Wood started forward about 1700, driving a Confederate cavalry screen northeastward over Pickett's Mill Creek. But Wood soon encountered trouble in the form of Cleburne's division—arguably the finest combat unit in Johnston's army—which held the high ground to the south. Wood's lead brigade attacked Cleburne's strong position and withdrew after suffering over 500 casualties in a matter of minutes. The Union assault at Pickett's Mill deteriorated into a series of disjointed attacks that succeeded only in raising the Federal casualty count to 1,600, while the rebels lost less than one-third that amount.

Seeking to capitalize on Cleburne's success, Johnston sent Hood's corps on a night march around the Union left flank to launch a surprise attack the next morning. As at Cassville, Hood found Federals where he had not expected them and so informed Johnston, who canceled the assault. This disappointing episode further widened the gulf that now separated Johnston and Hood.

Sherman likewise had problems with two sizable gaps in the Union line—one between McPherson and Thomas and the other between Schofield and Howard. He decided to fill the holes while shifting northeast toward the Western and Atlantic. Johnston soon discerned Sherman's intent and, on 28 May, launched his first assault of the campaign to pin down the Federals in the Dallas area. Elements of Hardee's corps and Jackson's cavalry division harried but ultimately were unable to halt McPherson's advance toward the railroad. The Confederates' failure was not due to a lack of effort. According to an Illinois captain, "a heavy column of Rebels rose from a brush with a yell the devil ought to copyright"—no doubt the infamous rebel yell. The soldiers in gray captured some Union guns and then lost them when the Federals counterattacked in force.

On 1 June, Federal cavalry seized the now-vacant Allatoona Pass. Two days later, the Union advance reached Acworth on the Western and Atlantic, and the Federals caught their first glimpse of Kennesaw Mountain towering above the mist to the south. Spirits rose in Sherman's army group, for they had regained the railroad and had left the Hell Hole far behind. The Union chieftain gave his men a few days' rest while his engineers repaired the Etowah River railroad bridge, before resuming the march toward Atlanta.

Just beyond Kennesaw Mountain lay Marietta, Georgia, a flourishing railroad town. Thirty miles farther south stood the city of Atlanta. To reach its geographical objective, Sherman's army group would first have to cross two mountain ranges and then the Chattahoochee River. Sherman chose the Sandtown Road as his axis of advance. The former Indian trail wound generally southeast from Allatoona Pass to the Chattahoochee River and beyond, intersecting with most of the region's major roads along the way. The first mountain range the Federals encountered consisted of Brush Mountain and Pine Mountain—each 300 feet tall—and Lost Mountain, the tallest of the trio at 500 feet. Just beyond that range stood Kennesaw Mountain, composed of two large peaks and one spur: Big Kennesaw (700 feet), Little Kennesaw (400 feet), and Pigeon Hill (220 feet). The Confederates posted signal stations on top of the mountains to monitor Federal troop movements toward Atlanta.

In early June, the Army of Tennessee received what would be its last substantial reinforcement of the campaign. As Johnston's army neared Atlanta, Georgia Governor Joseph E. Brown appointed Maj. Gen. Gustavus W. Smith field commander of the Georgia militia and directed the 2,000 state troops to guard the numerous bridges and ferries across the Chattahoochee. Though grateful for the reinforcement, Johnston was understandably dubious of the militia, which bore the nickname "Joe Brown's Pets" because many of them had received state exemptions from the Confederate Army. The addition of the Georgia militia boosted the Confederates' total strength to 72,000. In the meantime, the Federals received an even larger reinforcement. On 8 June, Maj. Gen. Francis P. Blair Jr.'s XVII Corps joined McPherson's Army of the Tennessee. Blair's 10,000 veteran troops raised the Union army group's total size to 106,000, offsetting most of May's casualties.

Johnston also pressed the Confederate War Department for cavalry raids against the Union supply line, while Sherman took steps to prevent Maj. Gen. Nathan B. Forrest's Confederate cavalry division from severing railroads in Tennessee. He directed that Brig. Gen. Samuel D. Sturgis lead a combined arms force of 8,000 men and 18 guns from Union-occupied Memphis, Tennessee, and draw Forrest into northeastern Mississippi. On 10 June, Forrest routed Sturgis' much larger force at Brice's Crossroads, Mississippi, but the Federals had prevented the Southern cavalry from interfering with Sherman's railroads for several critical weeks.

The Brush Mountain–Pine Mountain–Lost Mountain Line

On the evening of 9 June, Union cavalry had located the ten-mile Southern line extending along Brush, Pine, and Lost Mountains. Early the next morning, Federal infantry began deploying opposite Johnston's new line. McPherson occupied the left along the Western and Atlantic before Brush Mountain. In the center, Thomas faced Pine Mountain. Schofield held the Union right opposite Lost Mountain. Brig. Gen. Kenner Garrard's cavalry division protected the Federal left flank and scouted east toward the factory town of Roswell, Georgia. The troopers of General Stoneman's division covered the Union right, while Brig. Gen. Edward M. McCook's cavalry division guarded the rear. Two consecutive weeks of torrential rains had flooded roads, creeks, woods, and fields. One Federal soldier complained that "it beats all how much it rains here. We have had but little good weather since we started. . . . We get water in our trenches and the ground is wet all the time and of course we get wet too."

On Johnston's overextended line, Hood's corps held the Confederate right anchored on Brush Mountain, Polk's corps formed the center, and Hardee's corps occupied the left to Gilgal Church, while Maj. Gen. William B. Bate's division deployed on Pine Mountain, forming a salient about a mile in front of the main line. Not surprisingly, Bate's troops joked that they were being used as "Yankee bait." Wheeler's horsemen patrolled the army's right beyond Hood's line, while Jackson's dismounted troopers covered the extreme left to Lost Mountain.

Convinced that Johnston's army was too small to defend ten miles of fieldworks, Sherman directed his army commanders to press the enemy line at all points to detect any weaknesses. He described the resulting close-range fighting in the dense woods as "a big Indian war," while a Confederate foot soldier noted that "pickets on both sides kept up a continual firing, that sounded like ten thousand wood-choppers."

The threat to Bate's salient led Hardee, Bate's superior, to arrange a meeting with Johnston and Polk on Pine Mountain to observe the situation firsthand. On the morning of 14 June, the generals and their staff officers gathered along the crest. At the time, Sherman happened to be riding along the Federal line opposite the mountain. Noticing the conclave of Southern officers, he remarked, "How saucy they are!" and directed that a battery fire several rounds to break up the gathering. The guns of Capt. Peter Simonson's 5th Indiana Battery immediately roared into action, firing three rounds at a range of 600 yards. In addition to scattering the Confederate officers, one of the projectiles tore through Polk's chest, killing him instantly. (By a twist of fate, Simonson would be shot and killed by a sharpshooter just a few days later.) That night, Hardee withdrew Bate from his precarious position. When the Federals took possession of Pine Mountain the next morning, they found this message: "You damned Yankee sons of bitches have killed our old Gen. Polk."

Sherman, meanwhile, directed all his armies to continue pressing the Confederates relentlessly. On 15 June, Butterfield's XX Corps division advanced up the Sandtown Road on a reconnaissance in force and found Cleburne's division dug in along the Gilgal Church intersection. Butterfield launched a frontal assault that Cleburne's men repulsed with a

Lt. Gen. Leonidas Polk
(Valentine Richmond History Center)

lethal combination of musketry and artillery fire. Geary's XX Corps division attempted to succeed where Butterfield had failed but met with the same devastating result. At dusk the battered Federals dug in opposite Cleburne and waited. The Battle of Gilgal Church had cost the XX Corps about 650 casualties compared to Cleburne's 250 losses. It was becoming all too apparent that Union forces suffered whenever they ran up against Cleburne's division.

Elsewhere, the Federals fared much better. Schofield's XXIII Corps threatened to turn Johnston's left beyond Lost Mountain, while in McPherson's sector, Logan's XV Corps overran a line of rifle pits along the Confederate right at Brush Mountain, capturing several hundred soldiers of the 40th Alabama Infantry. Johnston realized that the flanks of his Brush Mountain–to–Lost Mountain line were compromised, and he began to evacuate the position at nightfall on 16 June. During the eastward withdrawal of Hardee's corps to the Mud Creek line, batteries of the XX and XXIII Corps pounded Cleburne's division with solid shot and shell, inflicting several casualties. Among the wounded was Brig. Gen. Lucius E. Polk, one of Cleburne's brigade commanders and the nephew of the late Lt. Gen. Leonidas Polk. The younger Polk's leg was so badly mangled that it had to be amputated, bringing his field service to an abrupt end.

The Mud Creek Line

While Polk's corps—now commanded by Maj. Gen. William W. Loring—and Hood's corps held their positions, Hardee's four divisions hastily dug in along the bluffs overlooking Mud Creek. The point where Loring's left joined Hardee's right became known as French's Salient, a vulnerable angle in Johnston's line that was occupied by Maj. Gen. Samuel G. French's division. Finding this position too weak, Johnston sent his chief engineer, Maj. Stephen W. Presstman, to locate more defensible terrain to the south. The twin peaks of Kennesaw Mountain so impressed Presstman that he designated a new defensive position along the imposing Kennesaw ridgeline.

The Confederates had an unlikely ally in the weather. As the heavy rains resumed, Sherman became increasingly anxious about the deteriorating tactical situation and impatient with the recent lack of progress. On 16 June, he confided to the Army chief of staff, Maj. Gen. Henry W. Halleck, that he was "now inclined to feign on both flanks and assault the center. It may cost us dear but in results would surpass an attempt to pass around. . . . If, by assaulting, I can break [Johnston's] line, I see no reason why it would not produce a decisive effect."

On 17 June, elements of the IV and XIV Corps bridged a flooded Mud Creek and prepared to strike French's salient. Hardee, meanwhile, attacked the Union bridgehead twice but failed to dislodge the Federals. On the next day, Thomas concentrated his artillery fire on French's position and then sent out a strong infantry force that scattered Confederate skirmishers screening both French's and Maj. Gen. William H. T. Walker's divisions. In the Battle of Latimer's Farm, the Federals inflicted over 200 Southern casualties yet failed to capture French's salient.

Writing to General Grant on 18 June, Sherman expressed frustration with his army group's sluggishness. "My chief source of trouble is with the Army of the Cumberland, which is dreadfully slow," Sherman grumbled.

> A fresh furrow in a plowed field will stop the whole column, and all begin to intrench. I have again and again tried to impress on Thomas that we must assail and not defend; we are [on] the offensive, and yet it seems the whole Army of the Cumberland is so habituated to be on the defensive that, from its commander down to the lowest private, I cannot get it out of their heads.

Even as Sherman complained about Thomas' lack of aggressiveness, Johnston decided that French's salient jeopardized his entire Mud Creek line. That night, he directed the Army of Tennessee to evacuate under cover of a rainstorm and withdraw to their new position on Kennesaw Mountain.

The Kennesaw Mountain Line

The following morning, 19 June, Federal skirmishers discovered that the Southerners had abandoned their fieldworks. Sherman ordered a pursuit, believing that Johnston was headed for the Chattahoochee River, but the Northerners quickly discovered that the Confederates were dug in along Johnston's Kennesaw Mountain line. Laid out in a six-mile arc, the position consisted of formidable entrenchments that blocked three main routes to Marietta—the Stilesboro, Burnt Hickory, and Dallas Roads. Wheeler's cavalry corps held the Confederate right flank, with

Kennesaw Mountain, with Federal fieldworks in foreground
(George N. Barnard, *Photographic Views of Sherman's Campaign*)

Hood's corps digging in on Wheeler's left. In the center, Loring's corps straddled the mountain from the Western and Atlantic southward to the Burnt Hickory Road. Hardee's corps stretched from Loring's left flank, crossed the Dallas Road, and ended on high ground overlooking swampy John Ward Creek. On the far left, Jackson's cavalry division patrolled the roads and ridges to the south. To the Federals, the Kennesaw Mountain line resembled a massive earthen fortress.

On the Union side, Garrard's cavalry division covered the left toward Marietta to the south and Roswell to the east. McPherson's Army of the Tennessee held the line opposite Hood, while Thomas' Army of the Cumberland occupied its usual position in the center, facing both Loring and Hardee. On the right, Schofield's Army of the Ohio, now functioning as Sherman's flying column, advanced along the Sandtown Road west of Noyes' Creek, approaching the Confederate left. McCook's cavalry division covered the far Union right toward the Chattahoochee.

Annoyed with the slow pace of his army group, on 20 June Sherman ordered Garrard to cross Noonday Creek and attack Wheeler. Col. Robert H. G. Minty's brigade was the first Federal cavalry across, and, to Minty's astonishment, Wheeler's entire command charged his lone brigade. The result was the largest cavalry engagement of the campaign. After a series of mounted saber charges and countercharges, the heavily outnumbered Minty retreated to Noonday Creek, where Federal artillery on the north bank and Col. Abraham Miller's famed "Lightning Brigade" of mounted infantry provided timely support. The cavalry clash resulted in about a hundred total casualties.

The Battle of Kolb's Farm

While most of the Federals kept a close watch on the Confederate entrenchments along Kennesaw Mountain, Hooker's XX Corps and Schofield's XXIII Corps spent 19–20 June probing for the Southern left flank amid heavy rains. On 21 June, the XX Corps approached the Powder Springs Road from the northwest and ultimately deployed on the north side of the road near Kolb's farmhouse. Meanwhile, the XXIII Corps headed down the Sandtown Road, crossing flooded Noyes' Creek, where Jackson's Confederate cavalry had removed planks from the bridge to delay the Union advance. Once over the creek, Schofield's two divisions separated. Brig. Gen. Milo S. Hascall's division marched straight ahead and formed on Hooker's right near the Kolb house. Brig. Gen. Jacob D. Cox's division continued south on the Sandtown Road to the intersection with the Powder Springs Road and then stretched northeastward from there, forming a line that faced south and comprised the Union right flank. Four miles to the southwest, Stoneman's cavalry division patrolled the area near Powder Springs.

Jackson's delaying action on Noyes' Creek had alerted Johnston to the threat to his left flank, which on 21 June extended only to John Ward Creek. That night, Johnston sent Hood's 11,000-man corps on a long march from its position on the Confederate right to the extreme left. Both Loring and Wheeler extended their lines to fill Hood's empty trenches. Hood's column passed through Marietta, heading southwest on the Powder Springs Road toward Hooker and Schofield. By the morning of 22 June, Hood had assembled his three divisions three miles southwest of Marietta on a north-south line straddling the Powder Springs Road at Mount Zion Church. Hindman's division held the right of Hood's line, with Stevenson's division manning the left and extending to the Powder Springs Road. Stewart's division formed in reserve behind Stevenson.

Johnston directed Hood to block the Federal advance on Marietta along the Powder Springs Road. Incorrectly believing that Hooker's three divisions constituted Sherman's right flank, Hood decided, apparently on his own, to deploy his corps to turn that flank with a vigorous attack. Uncertain of the situation along their front, Schofield and Hooker deployed one regiment each as skirmishers. The Federals entered the tree line east of the Kolb farmhouse and captured several prisoners, who revealed that Hood's corps occupied the woods just beyond. The skirmishers relayed this information to the main Union line, where Williams' XX Corps division occupied a ridge west of the Kolb house, stretching northward to John Ward Creek. From there, Geary's XX Corps division extended the line farther north toward the Dallas Road. On the XX Corps' right, Hascall's XXIII Corps division deployed along the Powder Springs Road facing southeast.

General Hood
(Hal Jespersen)

For the first time in almost a month, the skies cleared and the sun shone, promising favorable conditions for Hood's assault. At 1700 Hindman's and Stevenson's divisions emerged from the tree line arrayed in line of battle with few skirmishers, evidently because Hood expected to encounter minimal resistance. As a result, the Confederates were unaware, until it was too late, that the Federals had deployed forty pieces of artillery along their line. According to one skirmisher in blue, Sgt. Rice C. Bull of the 123d New York Infantry, the Federal guns opened fire with shot and shell as the Southern line swept into the Kolb Farm's thousand-yard-wide field, endangering friend and foe alike. "We were in their line of fire and for a time in as much danger from them as the enemy," Bull recalled, "so we tried to file off to the right and left out of range. Winded, we made a last effort and struggled through our lines. Everyone fell to the ground exhausted, and many were in a dead faint."

As the rebels moved to within close range, no fewer than five Union batteries hammered the gray and butternut line with case shot and canister. During the assault, Battery I, 1st New York Light Artillery, alone fired 669 rounds. Many of the attackers took shelter from the firestorm, using every available depression on that vast killing field. As Hindman's and Stevenson's assault collapsed, Stewart's division advanced on the left but came to a halt when it encountered Hascall's line, ending the attack. The Battle of Kolb's Farm cost the Confederates 1,000 casualties compared to the Federals' 350 losses. At nightfall, Hood withdrew to Mount Zion Church. Though badly managed, Hood's assault had blunted Sherman's flanking maneuver via the Powder Springs Road and bought precious time for the Confederate forces on the Kennesaw line. This latest setback further delayed Sherman's timetable, leading him to make a fateful decision: he would forgo another flank attack and launch a frontal assault instead.

In the meantime, Johnston's appeals to Richmond for a cavalry raid to sever Sherman's supply line seemed to bear fruit. On 20 June, a force of 1,600 Confederate cavalry under Brig. Gen. Gideon J. Pillow left Oxford, Alabama, to cut the Western and Atlantic Railroad between Chattanooga and Dalton. Four days later, Pillow attacked the Union garrison at La Fayette, Georgia, well short of his objective. He lacked artillery to batter the fortified buildings that the Northern troops were using for cover and reluctantly withdrew when Union reinforcements arrived, returning to Alabama without having reached the Western and Atlantic. For the moment, at least, the Federal supply line remained intact and fully operational, but Pillow's failed raid nevertheless reinforced Sherman's decision to attack.

The Battle of Kennesaw Mountain

Sherman was confident that Johnston's Kennesaw Mountain line was overextended and that launching simultaneous attacks on several key points would cause it to collapse and perhaps lead to a breakthrough that would end the campaign with one decisive blow. Sherman's plan was ambitious, to say the least. The Southern line now ran eight miles from the Canton Road north of Kennesaw Mountain to the Marietta-Sandtown Road south of Kolb's Farm. Sherman decided to stretch Johnston's line even farther by probing its flanks and then breaking the line at two points in the center.

On 24 June, he issued orders giving his subordinates three days to reconnoiter the enemy's lines, choose the points of attack, and deploy the assault units. Sherman designated the Army of the Cumberland to launch the main assault. Thomas' men would pierce the Confederate center along the Dallas Road and then seize the Western and Atlantic just south of Marietta. On Thomas' left, McPherson's Army of the Tennessee would support the main effort by puncturing the Confederate line just south of Pigeon Hill, advancing a strong skirmish line to carry the summit of Big Kennesaw, and sending a combined force of infantry and cavalry toward Marietta. On the Union right, Schofield's Army of the Ohio would conduct a diversion along the Powder Springs Road near the Kolb's Farm battlefield. Sherman set up his command post on a hill near the center of Thomas' line. To facilitate communication, he had telegraph wire strung to the headquarters of his three army commanders.

On 25 June, Schofield showed Sherman the obstacle he faced on the Union right: Hood's corps was strongly entrenched along its entire two-mile front. Schofield noted that a frontal assault on such a position would only waste soldiers' lives. Sherman agreed and modified Schofield's mission. The next day, two brigades from Cox's XXIII Corps division began probing the Olley's Creek area. One of the brigades crossed the creek unopposed, seized a hill, and dug in there, having turned Johnston's left flank. Johnston made no attempt to expel the lone Union brigade, leaving Schofield free to exploit the opportunity the next morning. As the sun set, Sherman's army group made frantic last-minute preparations for what the Union commander hoped would be the decisive battle of the campaign.

McPherson's Assault

Following an hour-long artillery barrage, McPherson's multipronged assault began at 0815 on 27 June. To the north, the attack on Marietta met with stiff resistance and soon stalled. In the center, elements of eight Union regiments, advancing in open order on Big Kennesaw, struck four veteran Confederate regiments. The combination of steep, rocky terrain and Confederate firepower proved too much for the Federal attackers, who nevertheless maintained a steady fire on the defenders. On the southern end, roughly 5,500 infantrymen from Logan's XV Corps attacked the Confederates dug in along Pigeon Hill. Brig. Gen. Morgan L. Smith's two brigades combined with one of Brig. Gen. William Harrow's brigades to form an assault force that hit the seam between Walker's division of Hardee's corps and French's division of Loring's corps, but the Federals could make little headway. Heavy artillery fire forced many soldiers in blue to take cover among the huge boulders. Some Confederate defenders even hurled rocks down at the attackers (*Map 3*).

McPherson's assault lasted barely two hours, resulting in 850 Union casualties compared to fewer than 300 Confederates. Sgt. Theodore F. Upson of the 100th Indiana Infantry noted that he and some of his comrades had become trapped in the no-man's-land separating the two forces at Pigeon Hill. "We were in a bad fix," Upson recalled. "We could not go ahead and could not get back. We took cover as best we could and kept up a desultory fire. . . . There we staid till night came. . . . Then, tired and discouraged, we fell back to a new line of works. . . . The assault had failed miserably along the whole line."

Thomas' Assault

A mile and a half to the south, General Thomas and his subordinates had made careful preparations for the Army of the Cumberland's part in the 27 June assault. Thomas and Howard, the IV Corps commander, had selected a hilly ridgeline along a tributary of John Ward Creek where the opposing armies stood just 330 yards apart. The two Union generals were unaware that the Confederate entrenchments on this part of the line happened to be flawed. The earthworks conformed to the actual crest of the hill rather than the military crest, resulting in "dead space" along the forward slope where attacking soldiers might find shelter. Maj. Gen. Benjamin F. Cheatham's division of Hardee's corps defended this part of the Confederate line, which included a salient that Southern soldiers dubbed the Dead Angle. Not surprisingly, it was on this part of the line that the dead space was located. Cleburne's division was dug in on Cheatham's right.

General Thomas
(Library of Congress)

A SKETCH OF THE
BATTLE OF KENNESAW MOUNTAIN
27 June 1864
Confederate Position
Confederate Entrenchments
Union Position
Union Attack
Union Feint and Demonstration
Western & Atlantic RR
Big Shanty
Brush Mountain-Lost Mountain Line
Brush Mountain
BLAIR
(XVII)
McPHERSON
DODGE
(XVI)
Kennesaw Mountain Line
Little Kennesaw
Mountain
Pine
Mountain
FEATHERSTON
WHEELER
LOGAN
(XV)
FRENCH
WALTHALL
LORING
Big Kennesaw Mountain
STILESBORO ROAD
Mud Creek
Noyes' Creek
Pigeon Hill
Marietta
Mud Creek Line
WALKER
BURNT HICKORY ROAD
THOMAS
HOWARD
(IV)
BATE
DALLAS ROAD
John Ward Creek
HARDEE
CLEBURNE
PALMER
(XIV)
CHEATHAM
POWDER SPRINGS
ROAD
"Dead Angle"
HINDMAN
HOOD
SANDTOWN
ROAD
STEVENSON
HOOKER
(XX)
Olley's Creek
MACLAND
ROAD
Kolb
SCHOFIELD
STEWART
JACKSON
(XXIII)

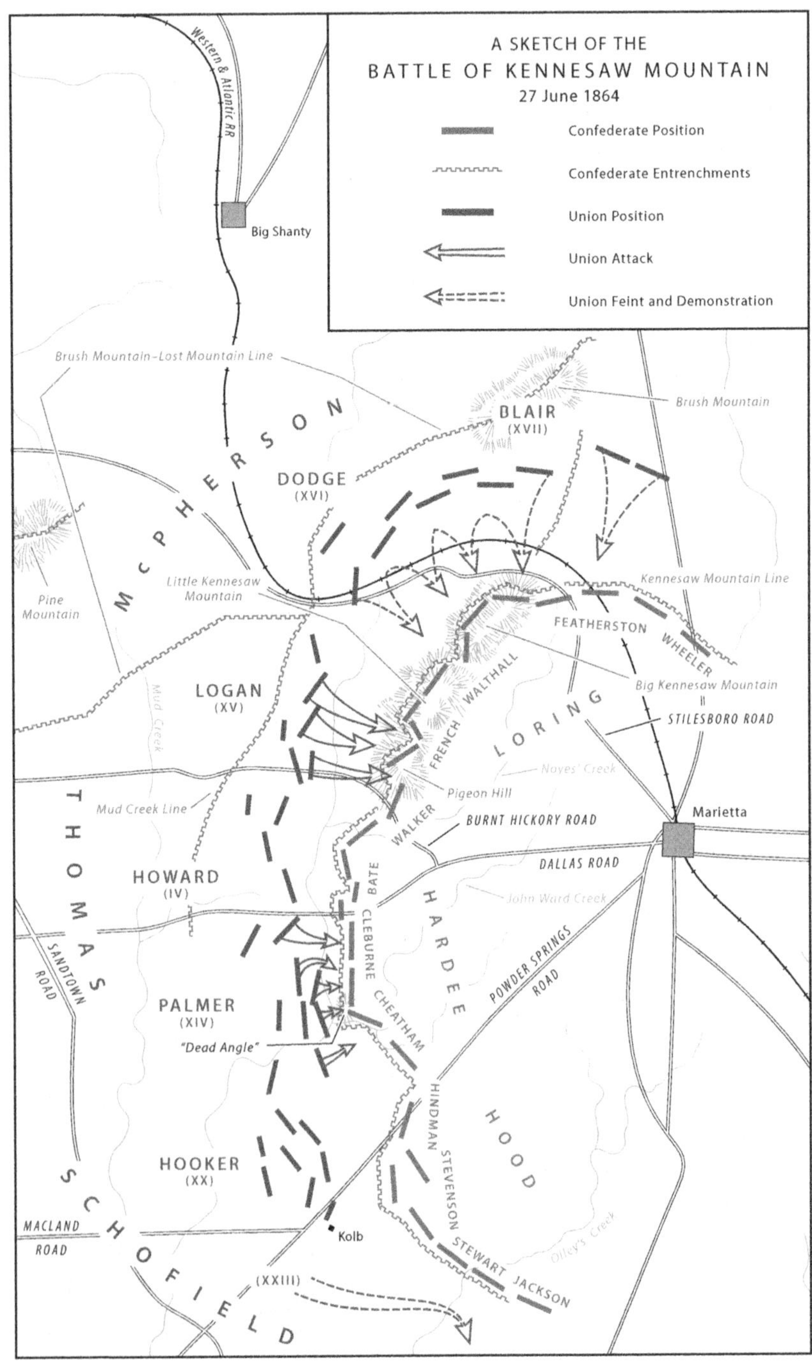

MAP 3

At 0900, nearly an hour behind schedule and after a token fifteen-minute artillery barrage, five Union brigades from the Army of the Cumberland left their trenches in densely packed columns and started downhill toward the stream. From there it was uphill to the waiting Confederates. Thomas' plan was for the assault troops to punch through the Southern line, and then he would feed reserve units into the opening. Speed was essential to the operation's success, with the assault columns under orders to cross the lethal middle ground without pausing to shoot. All three brigades from Brig. Gen. John Newton's IV Corps division attacked on the northern end, while two brigades from Brig. Gen. Jefferson C. Davis' XIV Corps division advanced to the south.

In Newton's division, only Brig. Gen. Charles G. Harker's brigade could make much headway, thanks to a draw that partially shielded the attackers from the deadly fire of Cleburne's division. Riding into battle on a fine white horse at the head of his troops, Harker made an easy target for enemy marksmen and fell mortally wounded. With their leader gone, the men of Harker's brigade lost heart and retreated without having reached Cleburne's line. In the meantime, a fire started in the fallen leaves and dry brush. The flames consumed some of the gravely wounded men of Harker's brigade, whose shrieks could be heard above the din of battle. On Cleburne's left, Lt. Col. William H. Martin, the commander of the 1st/15th Arkansas Consolidated Infantry, ascended the parapet waving a handkerchief as a flag of truce, the Confederate officer risking death to secure the rescue of wounded Federals from the woodland inferno.

Of Davis' assault force, only Col. Daniel McCook Jr.'s brigade reached Cheatham's line. McCook himself was mortally wounded as he tried to enter the Confederate works near the Dead Angle, where Pvt. Sam R. Watkins and his comrades of the 1st/27th Tennessee Consolidated Infantry were fighting for survival. "Column after column of Federal soldiers were crowded upon that line," Watkins recalled,

> a solid line of blazing fire . . . from the muzzles of the Yankee guns being poured right into our faces, singeing our hair and clothes, the hot blood of our dead and wounded spurting on us, the blinding smoke and stifling atmosphere filling our eyes and mouths. . . . My gun became so hot that frequently the powder would flash before I could ram home the ball. . . . There was

not a single man in the company who was not wounded, or had holes shot through his hat and clothing.

The Confederate batteries posted behind the Dead Angle enfiladed Davis' two brigades at short range with canister and case shot. Rather than run the gauntlet back to the main line, some of the Federals retreated downhill about thirty yards to the dead space, where they dug frantically with every available implement, including their bare hands.

By noon, it was clear that Thomas' attack had also failed. Although the four Union assault divisions had not broken through any part of Johnston's line, they still held some forward positions. In a flurry of telegraphic messages, Sherman queried Thomas on their options, indicating his preference for another attack. But Thomas refused to acquiesce: "We have already lost heavily to-day without gaining any material advantage; one or two more such assaults would use up this army."

While the main attack sputtered out, Schofield's XXIII Corps pushed far beyond the Confederate left flank, until the Federal advance stood closer to Atlanta than did Johnston's army. To the south of Schofield, Stoneman's cavalry division had moved to within five miles of the Chattahoochee River. Sherman rightly called Schofield's efforts of 27 June "the only advantage of the day."

General Schofield
(Library of Congress)

Sherman reluctantly concluded that his bid to end the campaign with one decisive battle had failed. He resumed his usual flanking tactics, shifting more troops to the right and collecting supplies to support them. In the meantime, a truce on 29 June enabled the Northerners to gather their wounded and bury their dead. The Battle of Kennesaw Mountain had cost the Union about 3,000 casualties and the Confederates roughly 1,000—the largest one-day casualty count of the campaign thus far.

In the aftermath of his Kennesaw Mountain triumph, Johnston received visits from two Confederate senators, who indicated that President Davis was tiring of the general's passive strategy of withdrawing from one defensive position to another without bringing Sherman to battle. In response, the Confederate commander renewed his plea for Davis to send cavalrymen such as Forrest and Brig. Gen. John H. Morgan on raids to sever Federal lines of communications north of Chattanooga. Anticipating this possibility, Sherman had already planned to send another expeditionary force from Memphis to keep Forrest occupied. Johnston's reliance on outside assistance thus left him dependent on circumstances beyond his control. Had he adopted a more aggressive strategy in northern Georgia, at the very least he might have appeased Davis and disrupted Sherman's routine of flanking the Confederates out of their defensive lines at minimal cost to his forces.

The Smyrna Line

In resuming his flanking tactics, Sherman intended to pry Johnston out of the Kennesaw line through maneuver rather than brute force. Once again, McPherson's army would lead the way, advancing beyond Schofield's right toward the Chattahoochee River. Garrard's cavalry division would occupy McPherson's trenches, while Stoneman's horsemen continued to patrol the Chattahoochee to the mouth of Sweet Water Creek. McPherson's drive to the river began on the night of 2 July, with his wagons carrying ten days' rations for the soldiers and forage for the horses. Notified of Federal movement beyond his left flank, Johnston immediately issued evacuation orders. He transferred his supplies to the Chattahoochee, wrecked the Western and Atlantic from Kennesaw Mountain to Marietta, and withdrew his three infantry corps, posting Wheeler's cavalry as a rear guard to delay the Federal pursuit. The Kennesaw Mountain defensive line had served the Confederates well, enabling them to stall the Union offensive for two weeks and repulse a full-scale frontal assault while inflicting disproportionate casualties.

On the morning of 3 July, Union skirmishers found the Southern trenches empty. Sherman pursued the enemy, intending to strike the Confederates while they were crossing the Chattahoochee. The Federals crowded onto all available roads leading toward Marietta, with Thomas' army advancing on the left along the Western and Atlantic, Schofield marching in the center, and McPherson moving on the right. About four miles southeast of Marietta, the rebels had used slave labor to build a six-mile line of fieldworks running from Nickajack Creek on the Southern left to Rottenwood Creek on the right. The line crossed the Western and Atlantic Railroad at Smyrna Station.

Sherman planned to launch a diversionary attack on Johnston's center while turning his left flank. Confident that his adversary would evacuate the Smyrna line without a fight, Sherman predicted, "No general, such as [Johnston], would invite battle with the Chattahoochee behind him." He was mistaken. Loring's corps held the right of the Confederate line, Hardee's corps occupied the center, and Hood's corps was dug in on the left. The Confederate infantry was augmented by several hundred of Smith's Georgia militia. On the Fourth of July, Howard's IV Corps attacked Loring's position along the railroad but could make little headway. Although Dodge's XVI Corps captured some enemy rifle pits at Ruff's Mill on the rebel left, the Federals failed to penetrate Hood's main line. After learning that the Federals were turning his flank, Johnston evacuated the Smyrna line on the night of 4–5 July and withdrew his army four miles to an impressive line of fortifications along the north bank of the Chattahoochee River.

THE CHATTAHOOCHEE RIVER LINE

In mid-June, as the Confederates had begun to occupy the Kennesaw line, General Shoup, the Army of Tennessee's chief of artillery, approached Johnston with a proposal to construct a crescent-shaped line of earthworks that would cover the Western and Atlantic Railroad bridge spanning the Chattahoochee. Johnston gave his approval, and Shoup immediately set to work, directing a team of engineer officers who in turn supervised about 1,000 slave laborers. In just one week, they built a marvel of military engineering, a five-mile-long fortified bridgehead featuring a series of mutually supporting, arrowhead-shaped redoubts later dubbed Shoupades after their designer. The fortifications were situated along a chain of hills running from the railroad bridge to Mason and Turner's Ferry. Shoup had intended for his entrenchments to be held by a relatively small force, freeing the bulk of Johnston's army for offensive operations. But Johnston violated the designer's intent by adding two miles of trenches on the left along high ground extending to Nickajack Creek and then by squeezing most of the Army of Tennessee into the extended line.

When the Federals reached Johnston's new line on 5 July, Sherman considered attacking but his chief engineer, Capt. Orlando M. Poe, wisely cautioned against a frontal assault. Sherman heeded Poe's advice, avoiding what could have been an even bloodier repulse than had occurred at Kennesaw Mountain. Instead, Thomas deployed astride the railroad on the left, McPherson moved into position on the right, and Schofield formed in reserve. Sherman and a number of other Union officers—including Maj. James A. Connolly, a XIV Corps staff officer—climbed nearby Mount Wilkinson to study the Chattahoochee River line. The officers got a far better view than they had anticipated. "Mine eyes have beheld the promised land . . . of Atlanta," Connolly later wrote, "glittering in the sunlight before us, and only 8 miles distant." The major watched Sherman "stepping nervously about, his eyes sparkling and his face aglow—casting a single glance at Atlanta, another at the River, and a dozen at the surrounding valley to see where he could best cross the River, how best he could flank them" (*Map 4*).

Sherman kept Thomas opposite Johnston to hold the Confederates in place, while McPherson threatened to ford near Sweet Water Creek, and Schofield searched for a crossing point between the railroad and the town of Roswell, some twenty miles north of Atlanta, where Sherman had sent Garrard's cavalry division to save the bridge across the Chattahoochee. When Garrard reported that the bridge there was already burned, Sherman turned his attention to Schofield, who chose Isom's Ferry at Soap Creek, roughly midway between Atlanta and Roswell, as the best place to traverse. The Confederates lightly defended the south bank of the Chattahoochee there, and that part of the river passed between high hills, concealing the Federals and their pontoon train.

At 1530 on 8 July, an infantry regiment from Cox's XXIII Corps division began to cross the river upstream, using a stone fish dam submerged by heavy rains. A half hour later, Hascall's division of the same corps started rowing across the stream in pontoon boats. The surprised defenders fired a few token shots and then fled at the sight of growing numbers of Union troops. By dusk, with one pontoon bridge completed, Cox finished traversing the river and began entrenching on high ground. The Confederates, meanwhile, made no attempt to counterattack Schofield's bridge-head. Early the next morning, Garrard's troopers seized Roswell's textile factories. The Northern cavalrymen burned most of the

Chattahoochee River
Peachtree Creek
BATTLE OF PEACHTREE
20 July
Howell's Mill
Col
Mt. Zion Church
Western & Atlantic RR
Mason and Turner's Ferry
Proctor's Creek
Elliott's Mill
LICKSKILLET ROAD
Ezra Church
BATTLE OF EZRA CHURCH
28 July
ATLANTA
North Fork of Utoy Creek
Railroad Defense Line
SANDTOWN ROAD
Macon & Western RR
Utoy P. O.
to East Point

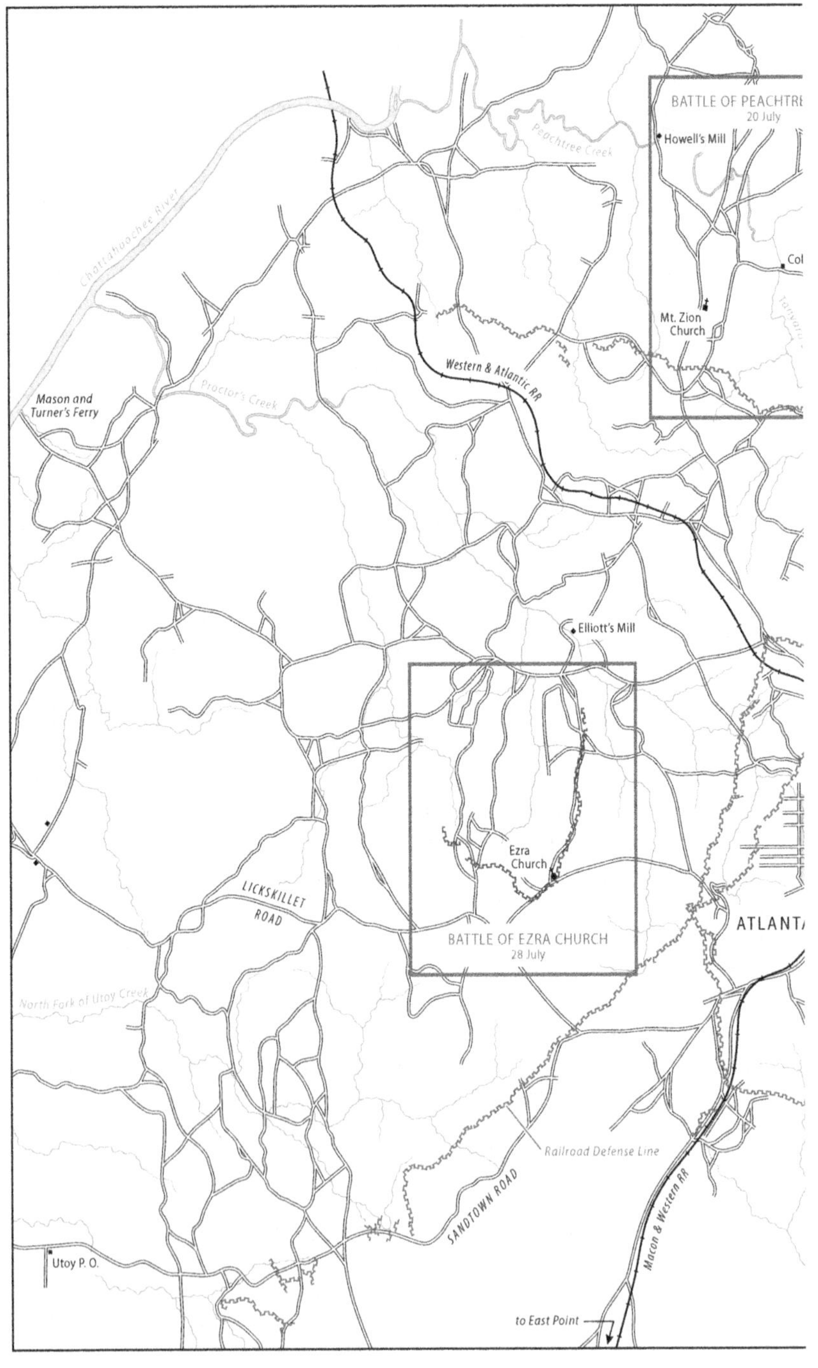

MAP 4

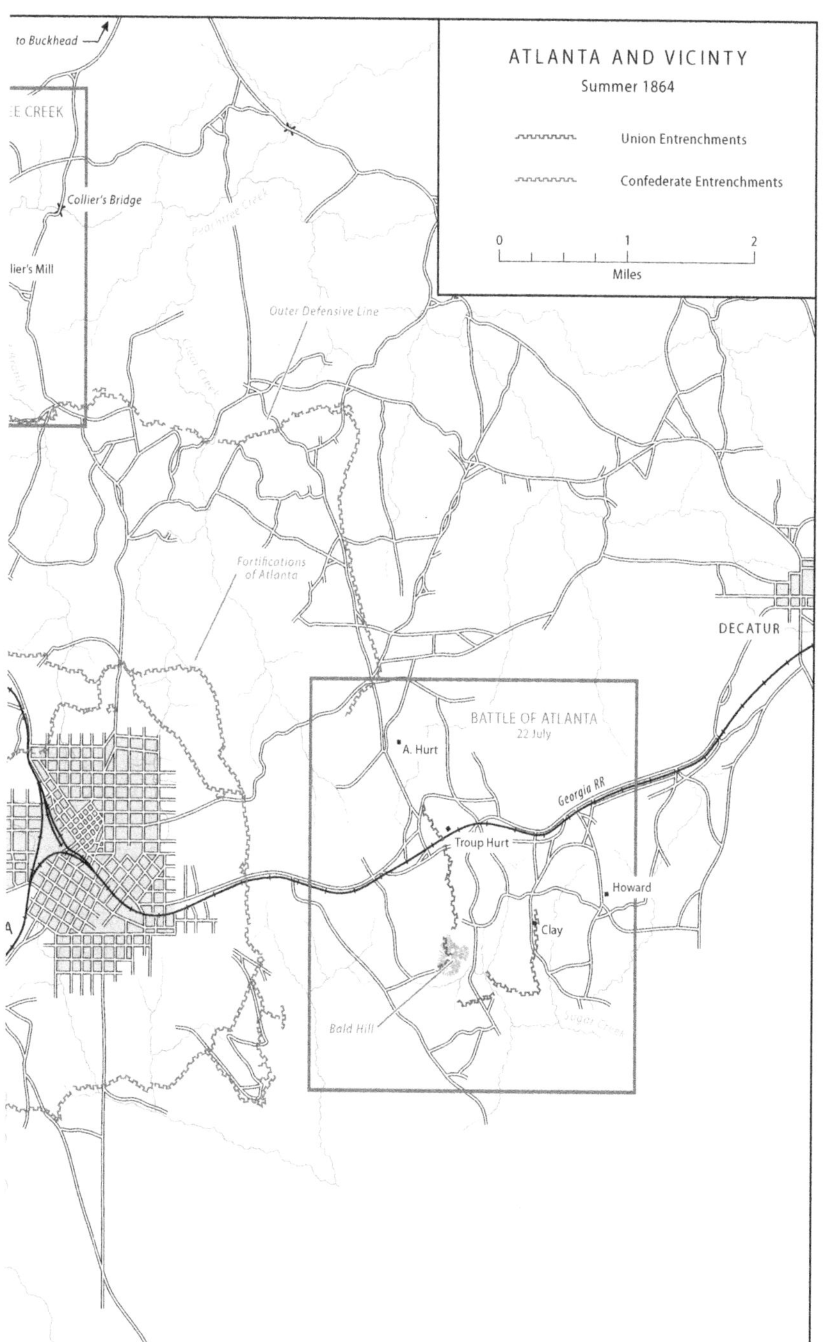

ATLANTA AND VICINTY
Summer 1864

Union Entrenchments
Confederate Entrenchments

0
1
2
Miles

to Buckhead
EE CREEK
Collier's Bridge
lier's Mill
Peachtree Creek
Outer Defensive Line
Fortifications
of Atlanta
DECATUR
BATTLE OF ATLANTA
22 July
A. Hurt
Georgia RR
Troup Hurt
Howard
Clay
Bald Hill
Sugar Creek
A

factory buildings and then transported the now-unemployed female workers to the rear. From there, the women were sent north to find work. His mission at Roswell accomplished, Garrard forded the Chattahoochee. The entire effort to gain the south bank of the river cost the Federals fewer than a dozen casualties.

The Union river crossings north of Atlanta compelled Johnston to abandon the Chattahoochee River line. Shoup was despondent, for his magnificent fortifications had not been put to the test. By the morning of 10 July, the Army of Tennessee had reached the south bank of the Chattahoochee, having destroyed the railroad and nearby wagon bridges. As the rebels withdrew toward the earthworks ringing Atlanta, Sherman's army group paused to rest and resupply. In addition, the railroad had to be repaired, bridges had to be rebuilt, and crossing points strengthened prior to the final drive on the Gate City. But the Union commander was already planning his next move. "Instead of attacking Atlanta direct, or any of its forts," he noted, "I propose to make a circuit, destroying all its railroads. This is a delicate movement, and must be done with caution."

A Change in Commanders

Deeply dissatisfied with Johnston's conduct of the campaign thus far, President Davis sent his military adviser, General Braxton Bragg, to Atlanta in mid-July to assess the situation there. In a conference with Bragg, Johnston repeated much of what he had already told Davis—that he refused to assume the offensive because he was heavily outnumbered and that the surest way to defeat Sherman was to cut his line of communications, thereby forcing him to abandon the campaign for want of supplies. Johnston further maintained that Forrest was the best choice for the mission because he could not spare Wheeler's cavalry. No friend of Johnston—who had succeeded him as commander of the Army of Tennessee—Bragg informed Davis, "I cannot learn that he has any more plan for the future than he has had in the past." Bragg further recommended that Hood replace Johnston.

Still uncertain as to his course of action, Davis consulted the South's greatest field commander, General Robert E. Lee, who advised against the proposed command change while in the midst of a campaign. The president tried once more to goad Johnston into action, but the general replied that "as the enemy has double our number, we must be on the defensive. My plan of operations must, therefore, depend upon that of the enemy. It is mainly to watch for an opportunity to fight to advantage." Davis had heard enough. On 17 July, as directed, Confederate Adjutant General Samuel Cooper sent the following message to Johnston: "As you have failed to arrest the advance of the enemy . . . and express no confidence that you can defeat or repel him, you are hereby relieved from . . . command."

Davis appointed Hood to replace Johnston and to assume the temporary rank of full general pending congressional approval. Just thirty-three, Hood had earned a reputation in the Eastern Theater as a hard-hitting brigade and division commander. His physical appearance only enhanced that image, battlefield wounds having disabled an arm and cost him a leg. Hood was as ambitious as he was aggressive and had schemed with Bragg to secure the army command. Well aware of Hood's propensity for recklessness, Confederate Secretary of War James A. Seddon cautioned him to "be wary no less than bold. It may yet be practicable to cut the communication of the enemy or find or make an opportunity of equal encounter whether he moves east or west."

While Hood assumed command, the roughly 55,000 soldiers constituting the Army of Tennessee withdrew across Peachtree Creek and filed into the earthworks north and east of town. By the summer of 1864, Atlanta had become one of the most heavily fortified cities in the South, and its wartime population had mushroomed to over 20,000 civilians. In the spring of 1863, a failed Union cavalry raid to cut the Western and Atlantic Railroad in northern Georgia had convinced the city fathers to authorize a local engineer, Capt. Lemuel P. Grant, to design a system of fortifications around Atlanta. Under Grant's supervision, conscripted slaves had built a ten-mile circuit of entrenchments linking numerous redoubts capable of holding about one hundred large-caliber guns. The laborers had improved the fortifications by clearing fields of fire and placing various obstructions—including *chevaux-de-frise* and abatis—in front of the earthworks. These works—situated just over a mile from the city center—constituted the Confederates' final defensive line.

Sherman, meanwhile, resumed operations, sending Thomas on a direct line to Atlanta from the north via Peachtree Creek, while sending Schofield and McPherson on a more roundabout route to strike the Georgia Railroad east of the city. Federal troop strength then stood at just over 106,000. On 19 July, Sherman

Confederate defenses northwest of Atlanta
(George N. Barnard, *Photographic Views of Sherman's Campaign*)

learned of Hood's promotion and consulted with McPherson and Schofield, both of whom had known Hood while the three were cadets at the U.S. Military Academy. The two men agreed that the new Confederate commander was bold to the point of rashness, which Hood had demonstrated as recently as his impetuous attack at Kolb's Farm on 22 June.

While Sherman's army group moved on Atlanta, another Union expedition left Memphis in search of Forrest, the Confederacy's most elusive cavalryman. Maj. Gen. Andrew J. Smith led some 14,000 Federal infantry and cavalry and 24 pieces of artillery into northeastern Mississippi. On 13 July, Smith's command occupied a strong position west of Tupelo and repulsed a series of disjointed attacks launched by 8,000 Confederates under Lt. Gen. Stephen D. Lee. Forrest's cavalry division bore the brunt of the fighting, suffering 1,300 casualties, and Forrest himself was wounded in a rearguard action at Old Town Creek the following day. In the process, Smith had sidelined Forrest for several weeks and thus prevented him from raiding Sherman's supply line. But Smith's success was a double-edged sword. After all, Forrest had prevented the bulk of Smith's veteran XVI Corps from joining Sherman outside Atlanta.

On the morning of 20 July, the Confederates manning the trenches one mile south of Peachtree Creek anxiously awaited the order to attack the Federals crossing that stream. The men of the corps of newly promoted Lt. Gen. Alexander P. Stewart (formerly Polk's command) held the left of the Confederate line, their flank anchored on the Chattahoochee. Hardee's corps occupied the center, and Hood's corps under its acting commander, General Cheatham, faced east toward the Georgia Railroad and the town of Decatur. Farther east, Wheeler's dismounted cavalry was drawn up astride the railroad, opposing the Federals advancing from the direction of Decatur.

Hood's attack plan was both ambitious and complex. While Cheatham and Wheeler delayed the Federals to the east, Hardee and Stewart would attack en echelon from right to left, striking the Army of the Cumberland as it crossed Peachtree Creek and destroying it in the angle formed by the junction of the creek with the Chattahoochee. Though sound in concept, the assault required precise timing—with no fewer than seven Confederate divisions slated to attack in close succession (*Map 5*).

On 19 July, Thomas' army would have been vulnerable to such an attack. The Army of the Cumberland had spent most of

General Cheatham
(Library of Congress)

General Stewart
(North Carolina State Archives)

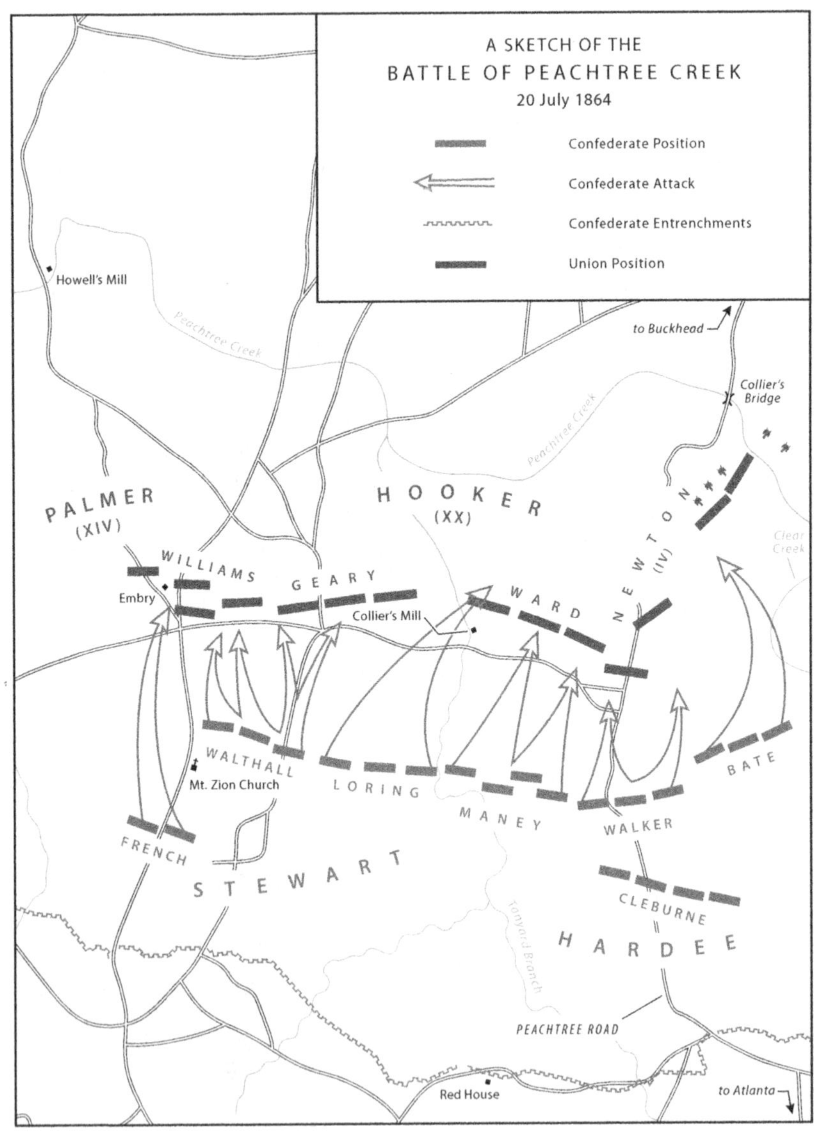

Map 5

that day crossing the creek, but by the next morning all units were across and digging in south of the stream. Even so, a two-mile gap separated Thomas from Schofield and McPherson—a situation that Hood sought to exploit.

At 0500 on 20 July, the entire Union line advanced a short distance, with Logan's XV Corps halting just two and a half miles east of Atlanta, enabling the four 20-pound Parrott rifles of Capt. Francis DeGress' Battery H, 1st Illinois Light Artillery, to fire the Federals' first salvo into the Gate City. Apparently killing no one, the shells damaged a few buildings and served notice that the city was under attack. Hood therefore postponed his assault from 1300 to 1530 in order to shift the entire rebel line to the right until Cheatham's corps straddled the railroad. Although the Southerners now blocked the Federal advance into Atlanta from the east, the delay had cost Hood valuable time.

Poor communication between Hardee's and Stewart's corps only made matters worse. The miscues began when Stewart's division at the far right under Loring launched its assault at 1445, about forty-five minutes ahead of schedule. Hardee's attack began on time at 1530, but Bate's division soon bogged down in the dense woods and underbrush in Clear Creek Valley. On Bate's left, Walker's division attacked along the Peachtree Road and briefly seized a section of the Union line held by Newton's IV Corps division. But General Thomas, a former artillery instructor at the U.S. Military Academy, directed the fire of several Northern batteries and thus helped repulse Walker's assault. To the left of Walker, Cheatham's division—now under Brig. Gen. George E. Maney—overlapped Newton's right, but the Federals managed to blunt Maney's flank attack. By 1800, Bate at last reached Newton's line, only to be driven back by U.S. artillery fire. Summoned by Hood, Cleburne's division left its reserve position and headed east to oppose the Federals approaching from that direction. With Cleburne's departure, Hardee had no more men to commit, and he broke off the attack.

On Stewart's front, Loring's division advanced farther than any other Confederate unit, its success due in part to the element of surprise achieved by the early start. Crossing the Tanyard Branch on the right and the Collier Road on the left, Loring's troops descended onto the Peachtree Creek floodplain and struck Brig. Gen. William T. Ward's (formerly Butterfield's) XX Corps division, which held firm despite a ferocious Confederate assault. To the west on high ground near Collier's Mill, the guns of Geary's XX Corps division raked Loring's open left flank with canister. On Loring's left, Maj. Gen. Edward C. Walthall's division swept around Geary's right, but Williams' XX Corps division countered by refusing its left flank and subjecting Walthall's exposed left to a lethal combination of musketry and artillery fire. According to one of Williams' men, Sergeant Bull of the 123d New York Infantry, "The enemy made five charges on our line, coming at times within one hundred feet; yet I did not see a single Johnnie. The clouds of smoke from the muskets of both sides and from [a nearby battery] poured down on us to hide everything but the flash of the enemy's guns that gave us their position." Stewart's division at the far left under French advanced but was only lightly engaged before withdrawing. By 1900 the battle was over. The rebel assault had failed to drive Thomas' army into the Chattahoochee.

The Battle of Peachtree Creek cost the attacking Confederates about 2,500 casualties, while the defending Federals lost 1,750. There were numerous reasons for the Southern defeat. Hood had left execution of his complex plan to his subordinates, and Hardee had sent his divisions forward in piecemeal fashion, exposing their flanks to devastating Union artillery fire. The Federals also held the advantage of defending high ground, forcing the Confederates to attack uphill and through heavy vegetation.

Hood's Second Sortie: The Battle of Atlanta

During the Peachtree Creek fight, Wheeler's cavalry had captured an elevation referred to as the Bald Hill, about two miles east of Atlanta, extending the Confederate outer line southward well below the Georgia Railroad. Early on the morning of 21 July, Cleburne's division also occupied the hill and began to dig in. Advancing from the east, Blair's two XVII Corps divisions drove the Confederates off Bald Hill. Then Lt. John Sullivan's 3d Ohio Light Battery unlimbered and began firing rounds into downtown Atlanta. The projectiles caused minimal physical damage, yet the explosions terrified the city's residents. To restore civilian morale, Hood decided to put an end to the Union army's long-range artillery fire while securing the Georgia Railroad.

On 21 July, Hood devised another elaborate assault to drive the Federals from the Gate City. Learning that McPherson's left flank had lost its cavalry screen—namely Garrard's division, which was tearing up the Georgia Railroad near Stone Mountain—Hood decided to launch a surprise attack on the Federals east of Atlanta. He designated Hardee's corps as the main strike force. That night, Hardee and two divisions of Wheeler's cavalry would make a night march to Decatur and assault McPherson's army from the rear while Cheatham attacked from the front, crushing the Federals in the jaws of the Confederate vise. In the meantime, Stewart's corps and Smith's Georgia militia would prevent Thomas and Schofield from coming to McPherson's rescue.

In the darkness Hardee's corps evacuated its trenches along Peachtree Creek and headed south, the weary soldiers trudging through the streets of Atlanta amid oppressive heat and choking dust. By the time the column had reached the revised jump-off point north and west of Terry's Mill Pond, it was noon on 22 July—hours behind schedule and well short of Decatur. But the men had marched fifteen miles, much of it under a hot sun, and were thoroughly fatigued, having spent the previous two days marching and fighting on little or no sleep. While Hardee's corps made its night march, Cheatham's corps filed out of its trenches east of Atlanta in preparation for the frontal assault on McPherson. Hardee and Cheatham's empty earthworks led Sherman to assume that Hood had abandoned Atlanta, but Thomas and Schofield reported that the rebels still occupied Atlanta's inner ring of fortifications.

On the morning of 22 July, the right and center of McPherson's line extended along a north-south axis, straddling both the Georgia Railroad and the Bald Hill. Earlier that morning, McPherson had received word of a large Confederate force moving east, so he refused his vulnerable left flank, facing General Dodge's two XVI Corps divisions southward on either side of Sugar Creek. Without knowing it, McPherson had placed the XVI Corps in an excellent position to block Hardee's impending assault (*Map 6*).

Just a few hundred yards south of the XVI Corps, Hardee launched his attack at 1215, and firing soon erupted as Union and Confederate skirmishers made contact along Sugar Creek. But the Southern assault lacked momentum, for the troops of Bate's division had earlier struggled across a swamp, and General Walker was killed before his division had even deployed. As a result, the XVI Corps divisions of Sweeny and Brig. Gen. John W. Fuller had little difficulty repulsing Hardee's two divisions at the far right.

On Hardee's left, Cleburne's division enjoyed initial success, exploiting a gap in the Union line between the right of the XVI Corps and the left of Blair's XVII Corps. As the enemy poured through the opening, McPherson and several of his staff officers were riding along that part of the line toward the threatened XVII Corps. The Union general blundered into soldiers of the 5th Confederate Infantry, who demanded that he surrender. Instead,

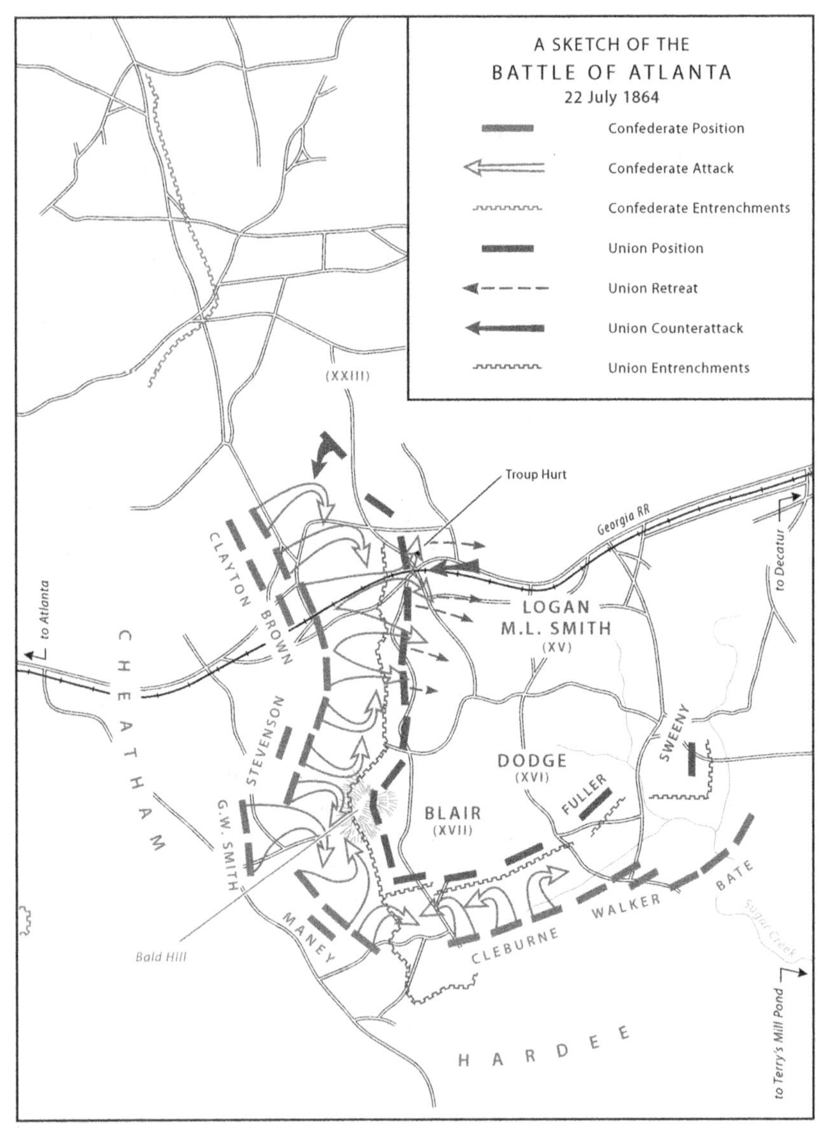

MAP 6

McPherson tipped his hat and attempted to escape but was shot down and died soon afterward—the only Union army commander to be killed in battle.

Pressing on, Cleburne's men struck the left flank and rear of the XVII Corps' line, held by Brig. Gen. Giles A. Smith's division. The fighting quickly became hand-to-hand with fixed bayonets and clubbed muskets. No sooner had Giles Smith's Federals driven back Cleburne's men, than Gustavus Smith's Georgia militia and Maney's division attacked from the front. The men of Smith's Union division repulsed Maney's onslaught, only to find that Cleburne was again attacking from the rear, while Maney launched yet another frontal assault. The combined pressure from front and rear forced the Federals of Smith's division back to Bald Hill, which was held by Brig. Gen. Mortimer D. Leggett's XVII Corps division.

On the Union right, meanwhile, Sherman could hear the din of battle to the south from his headquarters at the Howard house, located behind the Army of the Ohio's line. On receiving word of the death of his friend and protégé McPherson, Sherman designated General Logan as acting commander of the Army of the Tennessee, while Brig. Gen. Morgan L. Smith assumed temporary command of the XV Corps. Like Sherman, Hood could hear the fighting along the angle formed by the XVI Corps' and the XVII Corps' lines from his headquarters near Atlanta's City Burial Place. He misinterpreted the battle noise as evidence that Hardee had turned McPherson's left flank: the time seemed right to finish off the Federals. At 1500, Hood ordered Cheatham to strike the Union center, which was held by the XV Corps. Thirty minutes later, Cheatham's three divisions began their assault.

The attacks of Stevenson's division on the right and of Maj. Gen. Henry D. Clayton's division on the left soon faltered due to overwhelming Federal firepower. Sherman lent his support to the XV Corps' defensive effort. A former artilleryman, he directed the fire of five XXIII Corps batteries on Clayton's open left flank. In the center, however, Brig. Gen. John C. Brown's (formerly

General Logan
(Library of Congress)

Hindman's) division swept into the Georgia Railroad cut and routed the understrength Union force guarding it. Brown's onrushing Confederates captured the four guns of DeGress' battery and punched a hole in the Federal line that extended southward from near the Troup Hurt house to well below the railroad. The Army of the Tennessee's new commander, Black Jack Logan, reacted quickly to the breakthrough, personally leading a five-brigade counterattack that by 1700 had sealed the breach in the XV Corps' line.

In the meantime, the fighting raged on at Bald Hill, with Maney and Cleburne continuing to assail the XVII Corps' line. To prevent another Confederate flanking maneuver, Giles Smith's division formed on Leggett's left, facing south, while Col. Hugo Wangelin's XV Corps brigade filled the gap between Smith's left and the XVI Corps' right. The fighting was at close quarters and seesawed back and forth across the Union fieldworks. At one

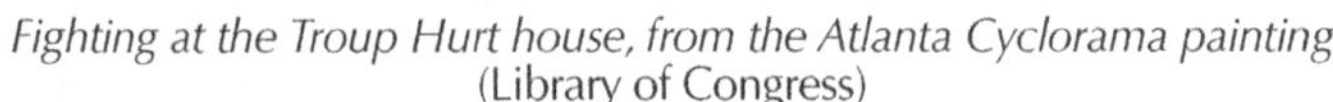

Fighting at the Troup Hurt house, from the Atlanta Cyclorama painting
(Library of Congress)

point, Col. William W. Belknap—the commander of the 15th Iowa Infantry and a future secretary of war—captured Col. Harris D. Lampley of the 45th Alabama Infantry by dragging him across the parapet. Private Watkins of the 1st/27th Consolidated Tennessee Infantry recalled Maney's final attack on Giles Smith's line:

> We gave one long, loud cheer, and commenced the charge. Like a mighty inundation . . . officers with drawn swords meet officers with drawn swords, and man to man meets man to man with bayonets and loaded guns. . . . Blood covered the ground, and the dense smoke filled our eyes, and ears, and faces. The groans of the wounded and dying rose above the thunder of battle.

His men collapsing from sheer exhaustion, Hardee ended the assault at nightfall. The XVII Corps' line had held. The Battle of Atlanta—also known as the Battle of Bald Hill—was over.

The 22 July battle was the costliest of the Atlanta Campaign. The attacking Confederates had suffered about 5,500 casualties and the defending Federals over 3,600. Two senior leaders, Union General McPherson and Confederate General Walker, lay dead. Hood's assault on the Army of the Tennessee had failed because he had demanded too much of Hardee's corps, the men nevertheless pushing themselves beyond all endurance, only to come up short at the end of the day. Credit should also go to McPherson's fortuitous troop deployments on the Union left flank, Logan's inspired generalship during the XV Corps' counterattack, and the grit and determination of the fighting men in blue.

More Command Changes

On 27 July, Sherman selected a new commander for the Army of the Tennessee. After consulting with Thomas, he chose General Howard, who commanded the IV Corps in Thomas' army. Howard also happened to be a professional soldier and a graduate of the U.S. Military Academy. Yet Sherman and Thomas knew the choice of Howard would rankle many both inside and outside the Army.

First, there was the matter of General Logan, whose superb performance on 22 July and long association with the Army of the Tennessee seemed to make him the logical choice. But Sherman and Thomas regarded the former Illinois congressman as a political general—a mere civilian in uniform. That left General Hooker,

General Howard
(Library of Congress)

the XX Corps commander, who was not only a professional, but who also happened to be senior in grade to everyone in Sherman's army group except Sherman and Thomas.

But Hooker had a history. The year before, he had commanded the Army of the Potomac in the Battle of Chancellorsville and had performed poorly. Although he had since proved himself as a corps commander, Thomas found him to be a difficult subordinate, inclined to lead his corps as if it were an independent command. Of course Howard also had a checkered past in the Army of the Potomac—his former command, the XI Corps, having been routed at both Chancellorsville, Virginia, and Gettysburg, Pennsylvania. That did not matter to Thomas, who found Howard easier to manage than Hooker. "You cannot do better than put Howard in command of that army," Thomas advised. "He is tractable, and we can get along with him." That was far more than could be said for Hooker.

In the end, Sherman's selection of Howard made him two enemies for life. One of them, Hooker, immediately tendered his resignation, which Sherman happily accepted. The other, Logan, resumed command of the XV Corps, but during the postwar years would become a formidable adversary in the halls of Congress. As for the IV Corps, Maj. Gen. David S. Stanley, the senior division commander, succeeded Howard, and General Williams became acting commander of the XX Corps.

In the meantime, Hood made several command changes of his own. He placed thirty-year-old Stephen D. Lee—the Confederate Army's youngest lieutenant general—in command of his former corps and returned Cheatham to his old division. Faced with a shortage of generals he deemed qualified for division command, Hood broke up the late Walker's division, attaching the four brigades to Hardee's three remaining divisions. Hood also replaced his chief engineer, Major Presstman, with the more experienced Maj. Gen. Martin L. Smith—a sure indication of the Confederate commander's intent to improve and expand the defensive fortifications surrounding Atlanta in preparation for a possible siege.

The Great Cavalry Raid

Sherman had no intention of storming Atlanta or laying siege to the city. Instead, he planned to cut the railroads bringing supplies and reinforcements to Hood's army. Sherman accordingly sent Garrard's cavalry division,

Lt. Gen. Stephen D. Lee
(Library of Congress)

already wrecking the Georgia Railroad near Stone Mountain, farther east, and, by the end of July, it had damaged the railroad to a point thirty-five miles east of Atlanta. In mid-July, Sherman also sent Maj. Gen. Lovell H. Rousseau's cavalry division on what proved to be a highly successful raid through Alabama and Georgia, during which his troopers destroyed a thirty-mile stretch of the Montgomery and West Point Railroad.

Garrard's and Rousseau's raids convinced Sherman that large-scale cavalry raids could do significant long-term damage to Confederate railroads. This was certainly true of the Montgomery and West Point, which in the aftermath of Rousseau's raid, was reduced to an eighty-mile spur line between West Point in western Georgia and East Point, a rail junction six miles south of Atlanta.

Sherman now focused on the Macon and Western Railroad, Atlanta's last major rail line. To break the Macon and Western—and thus force Hood to abandon the Gate City—Sherman devised an ambitious combined arms raid to seize East Point with Howard's army and to send a strong cavalry force to cut the railroad at Lovejoy's Station, about twenty miles to the south. Sherman assigned three of his four cavalry divisions to the expedition: Garrard's, McCook's, and Stoneman's.

Stoneman also persuaded Sherman to authorize a mission to rescue Union prisoners of war held at Macon and Andersonville, Georgia—a quixotic undertaking, to say the least, given the many thousands of inmates involved, their emaciated condition, and the considerable distance they would have to travel through hostile country. That Sherman would even consider such an expedition is astonishing, given his usual firm grasp of logistics, but the humanitarian dimension may have clouded his judgment.

The Great Cavalry Raid—as it came to be called with supreme irony—began on 27 July. From the start, Wheeler's Confederate cavalry kept a close watch on the Union mounted columns and prevented Garrard's division from making a rendezvous with Stoneman's division. McCook's division managed to reach Lovejoy's Station, where it damaged a few miles of track, but Wheeler caught up with McCook on 30 July and attacked him at Brown's Mill. Many of McCook's troopers were able to cut their way out, but over 1,300 Federals became casualties, while Wheeler's loss was less than 50.

Stoneman, meanwhile, ignored his primary mission and rode straight for Macon, where he found a motley force of state militia and local citizens led by Maj. Gen. Howell Cobb waiting for him on the outskirts of town. The unexpected reception thoroughly unnerved Stoneman. He abruptly aborted his rescue mission and headed back toward Atlanta. Confederate cavalry commanded by Brig. Gen. Alfred Iverson intercepted Stoneman's column at Sunshine Church, seventeen miles north of Macon. After several futile attempts at driving off Iverson's command, Stoneman sent most of his troopers riding hard to the north before surrendering the roughly 600-man remnant on 31 July.

The Great Cavalry Raid was a Union catastrophe. In addition to wrecking two

General Wheeler
(Meserve-Kunhardt Collection)

Federal cavalry divisions, the Confederates soon repaired the damage to the railroad at Lovejoy's Station. Adding insult to injury, the incident made Wheeler a hero in the South while Stoneman languished in captivity. The failed raid also convinced Sherman that only infantry could do a proper job of cutting the railroad.

Hood's Third Sortie: The Battle of Ezra Church

While the McCook-Stoneman raid was under way, Howard's army began its march toward East Point. As a diversion, Thomas and Schofield skirmished with the Confederates along their front. On 27 July, Howard's three corps reached the Ezra Church intersection, near the Lickskillet Road some three miles west of Atlanta. Howard's men began to entrench at nightfall, using wooden pews confiscated from the Methodist meetinghouse for building materials. The Federals occupied a fishhook-shaped line that faced east and south, with the barb near the crossroads. Sherman dispatched Davis' XIV Corps division to Howard's right in order to protect that flank, but the division became lost and wandered into the wilderness bordering the Chattahoochee River.

That evening, Hood ordered Stephen D. Lee and Stewart to move their corps on the Lickskillet Road to the Ezra Church intersection. The next morning, Lee was to launch a frontal assault to distract the Federals while Stewart turned their open right flank and pushed into the rear. But when Lee's first two divisions reached the intersection, they found a large Union force already dug in there. Under orders to occupy the crossroads, Lee decided to drive off the Federal intruders (*Map 7*).

At noon on 28 July, Brown's division attacked the right of Howard's line, which was held by Logan's XV Corps. Advancing unsupported through dense woods, Brown's troops could not see the XV Corps' position until they received a blast of musketry and a countercharge at close range. The dazed Confederate survivors turned and fled. Ten minutes later, Clayton's division assailed the XV Corps, whose lethal fire inflicted 50 percent casualties on two of Clayton's brigades. When told that the XV Corps was under attack, Sherman replied in his usual rapid-fire manner: "Good . . . that's fine . . . just what I wanted . . . just what I wanted, tell Howard to invite them to attack, it will save us trouble, save us trouble, they'll only beat their brains out, beat their brains out."

As Lee's two badly mauled divisions regrouped in the rear, two of Stewart's divisions marched to the sound of the guns. At

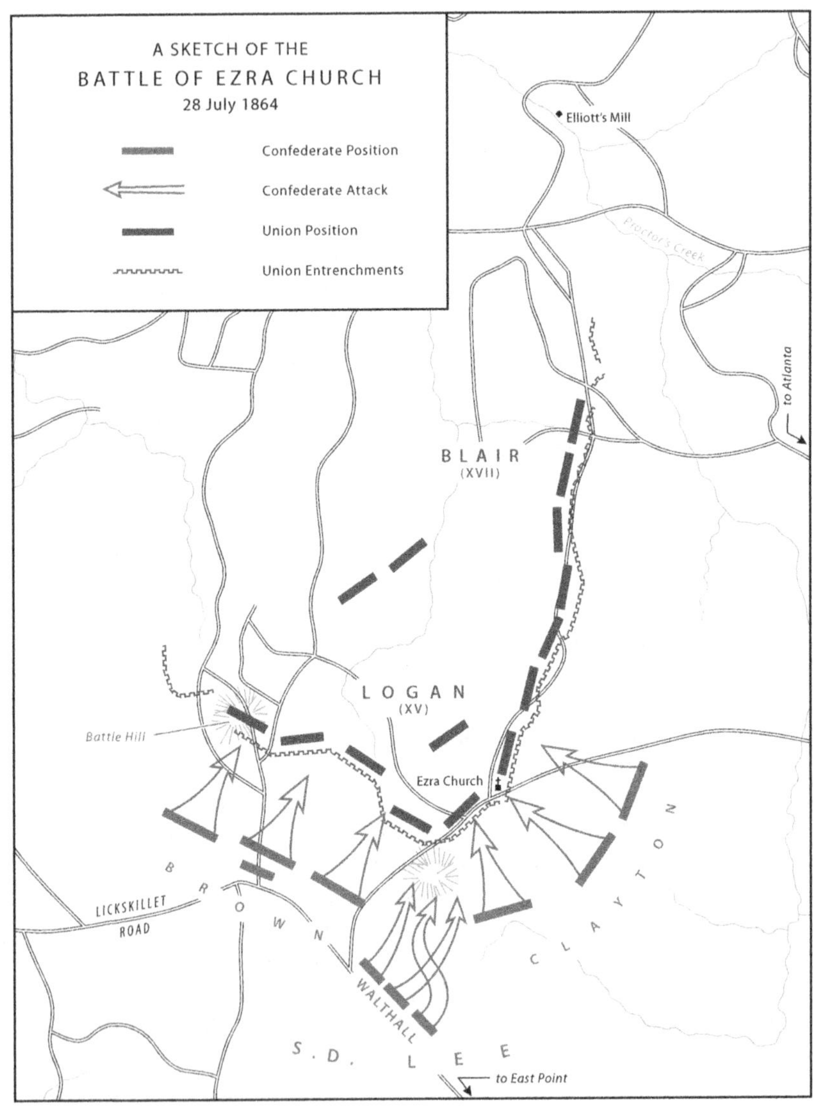

MAP 7

1400, Walthall's division attacked over the same ground as Brown's men and soon met with the same bloody result. Stewart then sent Loring's division forward to cover Walthall's retreat. About 1600, as the battle wound down, Stewart was struck in the head by a spent ball, knocking him unconscious and leaving Loring to oversee the withdrawal of Stewart's two divisions.

If nothing else, the Battle of Ezra Church had revealed that Stephen D. Lee ranked second to none—not even Hood—in impetuosity. Four hours of Confederate frontal assaults had generated about 3,000 casualties to the Federals' 650—a ratio of almost five to one. It was Kennesaw Mountain in reverse, more of a slaughter than a battle. Though poorly executed, the attacks had denied Sherman control of East Point—for now. The Federals may have held the field but they had not yet seized the crucial rail junction south of Atlanta.

Hood's three sorties had thus failed to drive the Federals from the gates of Atlanta. The assaults had proved costly to the Confederates, resulting in almost twice as many casualties as were sustained by Sherman's much larger army group. Hood had left the execution of his plans to subordinates who, for reasons largely beyond their control, failed to execute his grand designs. Perhaps he should have exercised more direct authority, but it is unlikely that even his intervention would have made much difference, given the Federals' numerical superiority. Although he had failed to defeat Sherman, Hood had given President Davis the battles that he wanted. And much more fighting remained to decide the fate of Atlanta.

Atlanta Under Fire

From the moment that the first Union battery moved to within range on 20 July, the city of Atlanta had been under a continuous fire. On some days, Northern artillery pounded the Gate City with as many as 5,000 rounds of explosive shell, solid shot, and even hot shot designed to set buildings on fire. The object was "to make the inside of Atlanta too hot to be endured," as Sherman phrased it. In August, the Federals brought in several siege-caliber guns and rained down more than 4,000 32-pound projectiles. And yet the five-week Union bombardment injured about a hundred civilians and killed twenty more, relatively low casualties considering the duration and intensity of the shelling. Even so, many inhabitants fled the city, while those who remained dug backyard bombproofs and endured the shelling as best they could. Defiant as ever, the Confederates replied with their own siege artillery that included a 9-inch Dahlgren smoothbore naval gun taken from the gunboat CSS *Chattahoochee.*

During the bombardment, Sherman continued to extend his line south toward East Point while probing the Confederate works for weaknesses. On 2 August, the Union commander shifted Schofield's army from the Union left to the right, deploying it along the north bank of Utoy Creek, about five miles southwest of Atlanta. Placing Schofield in command of a task force composed of Palmer's XIV Corps and Schofield's own XXIII Corps, Sherman ordered him to cut the railroad above East Point. But the attack was postponed when Palmer refused to take orders from Schofield, claiming that the latter was junior in rank to him. A political general, Palmer had grown tired of field service and seized on this dispute as a pretext for relinquishing his command.

The squabble over date of rank delayed the Union attack for several days, giving the Confederates ample time to strengthen their defenses. When Schofield finally launched his main assault on 6 August, it met with a bloody repulse at the hands of Bate's division, keeping Hood's last rail line open. The Battle of Utoy Creek cost the attacking Federals 1,000 casualties compared to the defending Confederates' 200. After the battle, Sherman accepted Palmer's resignation, and General Davis assumed command of the XIV Corps.

In late July, following his three failed sorties, Hood had decided to send Wheeler on a raid to cut Sherman's supply lines, an operation that his predecessor Johnston had deemed too risky to attempt. On 10 August, four days after the repulse of Schofield's assault at Utoy Creek, Wheeler led a force of 4,000 cavalrymen, most of Hood's mounted arm, northward to cut the Western and Atlantic, the Nashville and Chattanooga, and the Nashville and Decatur Railroads—a tall order for such a small force. Wheeler first struck the Western and Atlantic at several points between Marietta and Dalton, his troopers tearing up track and cutting telegraph lines. One week into the raid, Wheeler veered into eastern Tennessee to avoid Federal pursuit and to find forage for his horses, effectively removing himself from the theater of operations. On 17 August, Sherman informed Halleck of Wheeler's detour, noting that the Confederate raiders had "damaged us but little." The Union commander remarked that "East Tennessee . . . is a good place for him to break down his horses, and a poor place to steal new ones." The raid played right into Sherman's hands. By the end of August, Wheeler was riding through middle Tennessee but doing minimal damage to the railroads. He had failed to interrupt the flow of supplies to Sherman's army group, and his prolonged absence deprived Hood of his main reconnaissance force.

In the meantime, Sherman decided to give his cavalry one more chance to cut Hood's railroad lifeline. On 18 August, he sent his last fresh cavalry division under Brig. Gen. Judson Kilpatrick on a raid to sever the Macon and Western Railroad at Jonesboro, Georgia, seventeen miles south of Atlanta. Severely wounded at Resaca in May, Kilpatrick had just returned to duty and was eager to make his mark on the campaign. The Federals arrived at Jonesboro the next morning, and Kilpatrick's 4,700 troopers immediately set to work, tearing up three miles of track over several days. One Union soldier described the final stage of the process: "The ties are knocked loose from the rails," he wrote, "[and] made into piles, set on fire, and the rails laid on top. When they get red hot in the center about 20 men get hold of the ends and wind them edgewise around a telegraph pole or small tree. That fixes them." The bent rails were dubbed Sherman's Neckties. In this case, however, heavy rains prevented Kilpatrick's horse soldiers from heating the rails and twisting them into uselessness. Returning to Union lines on 22 August, Kilpatrick boasted that it would take the Confederates ten days to repair the damage he had done. By the next morning, the blaring of train whistles

An example of Sherman's Neckties
(Battles and Leaders of the Civil War)

to the south announced that they had put the railroad back in working order in just one day.

CUTTING HOOD'S LAST LIFELINE: THE BATTLE OF JONESBORO

Sherman once more turned to his infantry to break the railroad. On the evening of 25 August, he sent most of his army group marching south for Jonesboro, leaving only the XX Corps under its new commander, Maj. Gen. Henry W. Slocum, to guard the bridges across the Chattahoochee. On the morning of 26 August, Confederate pickets reported that the Federals had evacuated their trenches. This intelligence, combined with a report from Wheeler indicating that his raid had been a great success, led Hood to believe that Sherman was withdrawing from Atlanta due to a lack of supplies. But he soon learned that most of the Federals were southwest of the city and concluded that they intended to strike the Macon and Western. Hood posted Jackson's cavalry division on all the major roads below Atlanta to monitor Union movements there.

On the evening of 30 August, Jackson reported that Howard's Army of the Tennessee was nearing Jonesboro. Hood immediately directed Hardee to rush both his and Lee's corps to Jonesboro and, in an early morning attack, drive the Federals into the Flint River. Once that was accomplished, Lee would join Stewart and Smith's Georgia militia in Atlanta and assault the rest of Sherman's army group from the north while Hardee struck from the south. The ever aggressive Hood thus sought to seize the initiative even as he struggled to maintain his hold on Atlanta.

Although Hardee's corps—temporarily under Cleburne—reached Jonesboro on the morning of 31 August, Lee's corps had to make a longer march and did not start arriving until early that afternoon. As a result, Hardee had to postpone the attack to 1500. By then, Howard's army was dug in along a ridgeline about a mile west of the railroad at Jonesboro. The Confederates launched a series of disjointed and half-hearted assaults directed mainly at Logan's XV Corps. The result was a bloody fiasco for the Southerners, who suffered over 1,700 casualties compared to less than 200 for the Federals.

The news of Hardee's repulse had to be transmitted to Hood by courier because the Union IV, XIV, and XXIII Corps had seized the Macon and Western north of Jonesboro and had cut the telegraph line to Atlanta. Realizing that he had lost the railroad—and Atlanta with it—Hood summoned Lee's corps to the Gate City and directed Hardee to hold Jonesboro to cover the Army of Tennessee's retreat. Hood then ordered preparations for the evacuation of Atlanta to begin.

On the morning of 1 September, Sherman directed Stanley's IV Corps, followed by Schofield's XXIII Corps, to march down the railroad—wrecking the tracks as it advanced—and join Davis' XIV Corps in attacking Hardee at Jonesboro. Early that afternoon, Sherman realized that Lee's corps had left Jonesboro and instructed the IV Corps and the XIV Corps to strike Hardee's right flank at once. The Union assault began at 1600. Cleburne's division bore the brunt of the Federal onslaught and at first managed to repulse the Northerners. But three XIV Corps brigades assailed the angle in Cleburne's line held by Brig. Gen. Daniel C. Govan's Arkansas brigade and broke through. After a vicious hand-to-hand struggle, the Federals captured Govan and several hundred of his men. Somehow Hardee found enough troops to seal the breach and hold off the Federals until nightfall. Each side had sustained about 1,400 casualties.

That night, Hardee's men evacuated their trenches and withdrew to Lovejoy's Station. In the meantime, Lee's and Stewart's corps and the Georgia militia left Atlanta on the McDonough Road. During the evacuation, the Confederates put some boxcars filled with ammunition to the torch. The resulting explosions leveled several nearby buildings and could be heard as far away as Jonesboro. Sherman thought the distant rumbling indicated a battle in progress that might threaten Slocum at the Chattahoochee River. The next morning, he learned that Hardee had left Jonesboro and ordered a pursuit to Lovejoy's Station, where he found Hardee's corps well dug in. He decided not to attack until he knew the fate of Atlanta. On the morning of 3 September, Sherman received a message from Slocum reporting that the XX Corps had occupied Atlanta the previous day. Sherman immediately wired the news to Washington: "Atlanta is ours, and fairly won." As Hood's army concentrated at Lovejoy's Station, Sherman's forces began marching north toward the city. The Atlanta Campaign was over.

Hood Strikes North and Sherman Plans His Next Campaign

Arriving at Atlanta on 7 September, Sherman ordered the civilian population evacuated in order to shorten the city's defensive lines and to use the public buildings for storage and the private homes for living quarters. When Hood learned of the removal order, he fired off a letter of rebuke to Sherman. "Permit me to say," Hood wrote, "that the unprecedented measure you propose transcends, in studied and ingenious cruelty, all acts before brought to my attention in the dark history of war." Atlanta Mayor James M. Calhoun also wrote Sherman, asking that he revoke the evacuation order, but the general rebuffed him. "You cannot qualify war in harsher terms than I will," Sherman replied. "War is cruelty and you cannot refine it, and those who brought war into our country deserve all the curses and maledictions a people can pour out." During the occupation, the Federals removed about 3,000 civilians from Atlanta.

On 21 September, Hood moved the Army of Tennessee, since whittled down to about 40,000 troops, from Lovejoy's Station to Palmetto, Georgia, twenty-five miles southwest of Atlanta. Hood made the move to give his army a much-needed rest and to place it on the Atlanta and West Point Railroad, which now constituted his abbreviated supply line. While at Palmetto, President Davis came to discuss strategy and to deal with a feud that had erupted between Hood and Hardee, the senior corps commander. Davis reluctantly granted Hardee's request for a transfer, appointing him commander of the Department of South Carolina, Georgia, and Florida (*Map 8*).

Davis also had come to evaluate Hood's fitness to command. During the Atlanta Campaign, critics had accused Hood of wasting the lives of his men in reckless assaults. But Davis decided to retain Hood as commander of the Army of Tennessee, and he approved the general's plan to cut the Union supply line in northern Georgia and force Sherman to fight a battle on ground of Hood's own choosing.

Hood left Palmetto on 29 September, crossed the Chattahoochee River, and led the Army of Tennessee northward to strike the Western and Atlantic Railroad, Sherman's supply line between Chattanooga and Atlanta. To deal with Forrest and Hood—should the latter continue north into Tennessee—Sherman sent Thomas and two divisions to Nashville. On 5 October, Hood detached French's division to attack the main Union depot between Chattanooga and Atlanta, which was located at Allatoona Pass. The Federals under Brig. Gen. John M. Corse barely managed to hold out in a small, yet fierce, battle that resulted in over 1,400 total casualties out of 5,300 combatants. The Confederates met

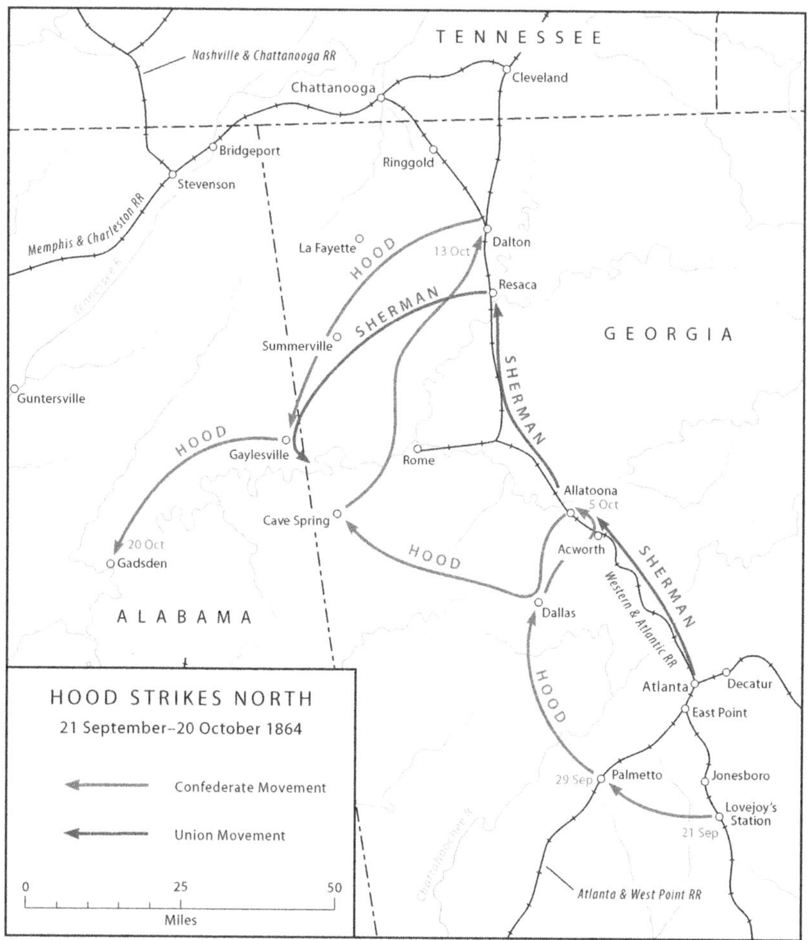

MAP 8

with greater success at Dalton, whose 800-man garrison surrendered without a fight. Sherman then pursued Hood's army along the railroad until mid-October, when it veered westward into northern Alabama. During the march, Hood decided on a far more audacious plan that involved defeating Thomas at Nashville before he could concentrate his scattered forces. Once that was accomplished, Hood would be free to enter Kentucky—perhaps sweeping as far north as the Ohio River—or head east to join Lee's army in Virginia.

Abandoning the chase at Gaylesville, Alabama, Sherman turned his attention to defending Tennessee and resuming his advance through Georgia. He sent Stanley's IV Corps and Schofield's XXIII Corps to Chattanooga and placed them under Thomas' command, while retaining the XIV and XX Corps under Slocum (newly promoted to army-level command), the XV and XVII Corps under Howard, and Kilpatrick's cavalry division at Atlanta.

For his next campaign, Sherman proposed to Grant a "March to the Sea" in which he would sever his cumbersome supply lines, move his army 250 miles to the Georgia coast, and capture the port city of Savannah. Sherman's army group would live off the land while damaging both the Confederate infrastructure and Southern morale. "I can make the march, and make Georgia howl!" Sherman assured Grant. "If we can march a well-appointed army right through this territory," he argued, "it is a demonstration to the world, foreign and domestic, that we have a power which [Jefferson] Davis cannot resist. This may not be war, but rather statesmanship." Grant gave his reluctant approval, and Sherman began preparing for the March to the Sea, trusting Thomas to defeat Hood while he headed to Savannah. In the meantime, President Lincoln won reelection by a landslide, dashing the hopes of many in the North and the South for a negotiated peace.

THE SAVANNAH CAMPAIGN

Before departing for the coast, Sherman ordered Captain Poe and the armies' engineer troops to demolish Atlanta's railroad and industrial facilities. The work of destruction began on 10 November. After reducing the buildings to rubble, Poe's men set the ruins aflame. The fires raged for almost a week, the conflagration spreading to the city's business and residential districts. According to XIV Corps staff officer Major Connolly, nighttime Atlanta "was bright as mid-day; the city . . . was one mass of flame, and the morrow

General Slocum
(Library of Congress)

must find it a mass of ruins. . . . All the pictures and verbal descriptions of hell I have ever seen never gave me half so vivid an idea of it, as did this flame wrapped city to-night."

Ever the perfectionist, Sherman oversaw the arrangements for the March to the Sea. He ordered all sick and wounded soldiers to the rear, leaving a core of 62,000 campaign-toughened veterans. He divided his army group into two wings. Howard commanded the Right Wing—or Army of the Tennessee—consisting of Maj. Gen. Peter J. Osterhaus' XV Corps (due to the upcoming presidential election, Logan was on leave stumping for Lincoln in Illinois) and Blair's XVII Corps. Slocum led the Left Wing—or Army of Georgia—composed of Davis' XIV Corps and Williams' XX Corps. Kilpatrick commanded the army group's lone cavalry division. To increase mobility, Sherman reduced the artillery to 68 guns. The supply trains consisted of just 2,500 wagons pulled by six mules each, as well as 600 ambulances drawn by two horses each. The wagons carried twenty days' rations and five days' forage, and a herd of 5,000 beef cattle accompanied the column. But these provisions alone failed to meet the Federals' minimum requirements.

In other words, Sherman's troops would live off the land. "The army will forage liberally on the country," the commanding general declared in Special Field Order 120. The order stipulated that brigade-level detachments would gather provisions far from the main columns—a suspension of strict discipline that Sherman deemed unavoidable. Having studied the Georgia census records for 1860, he knew that the region between Atlanta and Savannah could sustain his troops as long as they marched at a rate of ten to fifteen miles per day.

The Savannah Campaign began on the morning of 16 November. "We rode out of Atlanta by the Decatur road,"

General Kilpatrick, as a major general
(Library of Congress)

Sherman recalled. "Behind us lay Atlanta, smouldering and in ruins, the black smoke rising high in the air, and hanging like a pall over the ruined city. . . . Then we turned our horses' heads to the east [and] Atlanta . . . became a thing of the past." Sherman employed feints to keep the enemy guessing as to his intentions. Slocum's Left Wing headed eastward in the general direction of Augusta, Georgia, while Howard's Right Wing marched south toward Macon, with Kilpatrick's cavalry screening Howard's right flank. Sherman's actual objective, however, was Milledgeville, the state capital. For several days, the weather refused to cooperate. The rain fell in torrents and then turned to snow as temperatures plummeted. As a result, the roads soon became quagmires, slowing the Federals' progress to a crawl (*Map 9*).

An inevitable consequence of Sherman's march was the widespread confiscation and destruction of civilian property and the psychological devastation that resulted. Dolly Sumner Lunt Burge's ordeal was typical. A native New Englander who had married a wealthy Southern planter before the war, by November 1864, she was a widow managing a large plantation near Covington, on the Left Wing's route. She recalled the sudden arrival of a Union foraging detail:

> Like demons they rush in! My yards are full. To my smokehouse, my dairy, pantry, kitchen, and cellar, like famished wolves they come, breaking locks and whatever is in their way. The thousand pounds of meat in my smoke-house is gone in a twinkling, my flour, my meat, my lard, butter, eggs, pickles of various kinds . . . wine, jars, and jugs are all gone. My eighteen fat turkeys, my hens, chickens, and fowls, my young pigs, are shot down in my yard and hunted as if they were rebels themselves. Utterly powerless I ran out and appealed to the guard. "I cannot help you, Madam; it is orders." . . . I saw nothing before me but starvation.

In addition to the authorized foraging details, unauthorized bands of Union soldiers, or "bummers," traveled far from the main column seeking adventure and plunder. The bummers tended to deal more harshly with civilians than the legitimate foragers. Although relatively few of Sherman's men committed rape or murder, they nevertheless terrorized Burge and countless other civilians in their path—which was precisely what Sherman had intended.

Decatur
Atlanta
East Point
Covington
Madison
Orangeburg
Jonesboro
McDonough
Augusta
Jackson
SOUTH CAROLINA
MILLEDGEVILLE
WAYNESBORO
4 Dec
Thomas' Station
Louisville
BUCKHEAD CREEK
28 Nov
Clinton
Sandersville
Gordon
Millen
Macon
GRISWOLDVILLE
22 Nov
Sylvania
Camp Lawton
Swainsboro
Beaufort
Statesboro
GEORGIA
Savannah
FORT McALLISTER
13 Dec
Savannah R.
Ogeechee R.
Oconee R.
Ebenezer Cr.
Flint R.
XIV
XV
XVII
XX
UNION ADVANCE
MARCH TO THE SEA
16 November–21 December 1864
XIV — XX — LEFT WING Axis of Advance
XV — XVII — RIGHT WING Axis of Advance
Cavalry Axis of Advance
Battle
0   25   50
Miles

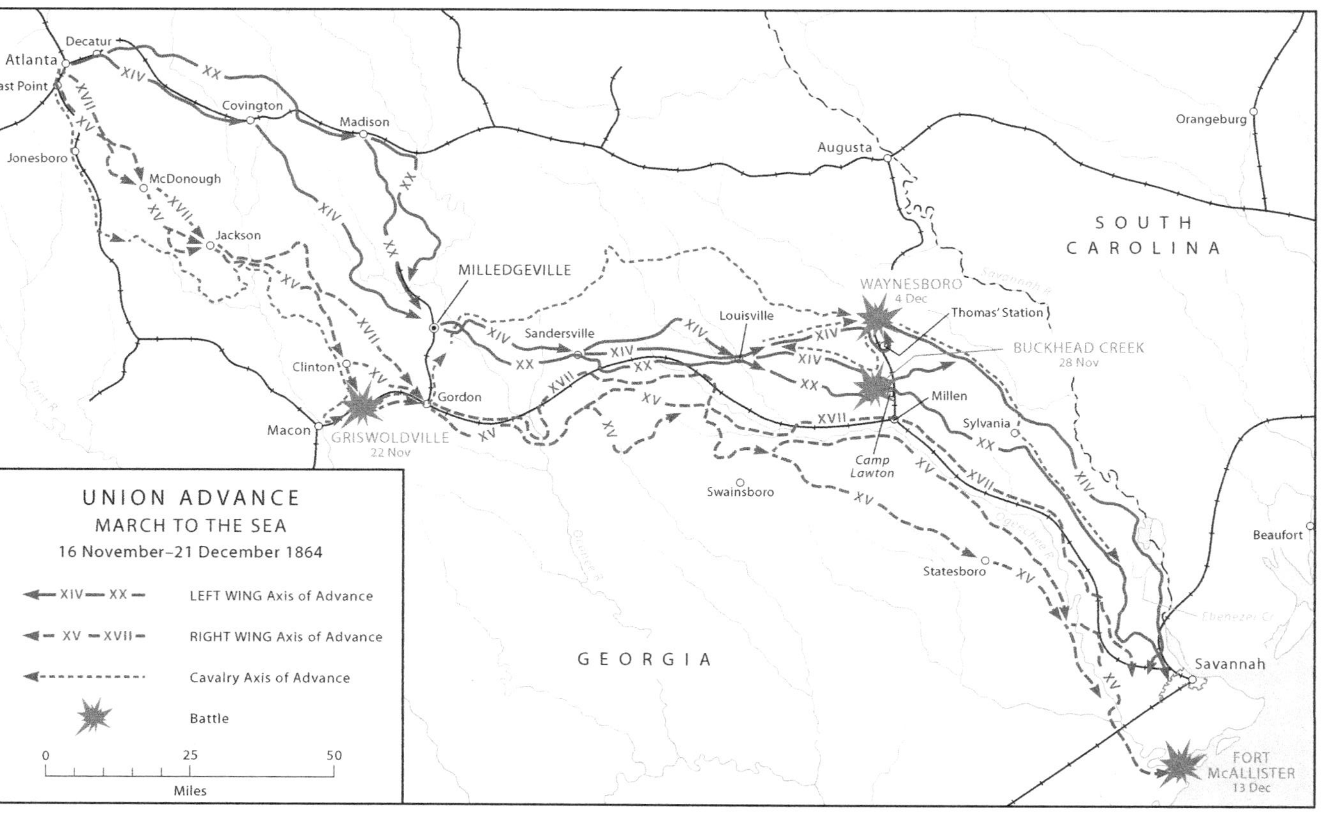

MAP 9

As the Union Right Wing marched south, General Hardee—the Confederate commander in Georgia—concluded that Macon was Sherman's next objective and began rushing troops to that point. On 19 November, Hardee boarded a train at Savannah and rode to Macon. He had roughly 15,000 men at his disposal, a motley collection that included Wheeler's cavalry, Smith's Georgia militia, and some local defense units. But when Howard's columns turned eastward the next day, Hardee decided that Augusta, with its arsenal and gunpowder works, was Sherman's objective. He therefore directed Wheeler and most of the Georgia militia to move there at once. Having set his forces in motion, Hardee returned to Savannah to strengthen its defenses.

The Battle of Griswoldville

On 22 November, three brigades of Georgia militia en route to Augusta from Macon passed through the smoking ruins of Griswoldville, a once-prosperous factory town, and beheld for the first time the devastation wrought by Sherman's army group. A mile and a half east of town, they collided with Federal troops deployed behind rail barricades. The commander of the militia, Brig. Gen. Pleasant J. Phillips, assumed that a small force of dismounted Union cavalry blocked the road. In reality, Phillips had come face to face with veteran Union infantry—namely the 1,500 soldiers of Brig. Gen. Charles C. Walcutt's XV Corps brigade—supported by a two-gun section of artillery and a pair of Kilpatrick's cavalry regiments. Walcutt had just driven off a detachment of Wheeler's cavalry, and, like Phillips, the Federal officer believed that his command faced only a small force of dismounted horsemen. Many of the Federals wielded Spencer or Henry repeating rifles, giving them an overwhelming fire-power advantage.

Phillips formed his command, which consisted mostly of ill-trained boys and old men, and ordered them to attack the Union position. Braving a murderous fire, the Georgians reached a ravine about seventy-five yards from Walcutt's position. From there, Phillips' militia launched three frontal assaults; when those failed, they attempted to outflank Walcutt's position but were repulsed by Kilpatrick's cavalry. They fell back to the ravine and then withdrew at nightfall. The outcome of the Battle of Griswoldville was predict-able: the Confederates suffered 650 casualties compared to fewer than 100 Federals, including Walcutt, who was severely wounded.

Afterward, Sergeant Upson and several comrades of the 100th Indiana Infantry "went down on the line where lay the dead of the Confederates. It was a terrible sight," Upson recalled. "It was a harvest of death."

Following the battle, the Right Wing resumed marching east toward the Oconee River, while the Left Wing neared Milledgeville and Kilpatrick's cavalry shifted to the left flank to shield it from Wheeler's cavalry. On the night of 22 November, Sherman—who was traveling with the Left Wing—made his headquarters at the Howell Cobb plantation. Sherman regarded Cobb, a former speaker of the U.S. House of Representatives, as the worst sort of traitor and ordered the men of Davis' XIV Corps to ransack his estate. The next morning, Sherman and the Left Wing entered Milledgeville. The Georgia state legislature having adjourned and fled, the Federals raised the U.S. flag over the statehouse and held a mock legislative session in which they repealed the state's ordinance of secession.

While Sherman's army group paused for a day of rest, several emaciated men staggered into one Union camp, saying that they had escaped from the notorious prisoner-of-war camp at Andersonville. Their arrival on Thanksgiving Day, as the Federals feasted on the bounty of the Georgia countryside, further underscored the suffering and deprivation the prisoners had endured. News of the Andersonville escapees spread rapidly, and, in the days that followed, smoke and fire marked the Union armies' lines of march, as vengeful soldiers torched barns and smokehouses and slaughtered farm animals. Sherman's bummers also escalated their violence against civilians, going so far in one case as to hang a plantation owner named Canning near Louisville, Georgia, until he lost consciousness. When revived, a terrified Canning surrendered small amounts of gold and silver in his possession. Wheeler's cavalry began to retaliate by shooting Federal prisoners, leading Sherman to warn Wheeler that he would execute one Confederate soldier for each one of his men so treated. The killings soon ceased.

The Federals left the rolling farmlands of the south-central piedmont and entered the flat, sandy, and swampy coastal plains region to the east. As the two Union wings converged on Millen, Georgia, Sherman directed Kilpatrick to rescue the Union prisoners held at Camp Lawton, five miles north of town. Kilpatrick began the expedition by feinting on Augusta to the north and then dashing south toward Millen, only to learn that the Federal prisoners had been transferred elsewhere. In the meantime, Wheeler's cavalry skirmished with the Union Left Wing's advance at Sandersville, Georgia, on 25–26 November and nearly captured Kilpatrick in a surprise attack at Buckhead Creek on 28 November, but U.S. horse artillery repulsed the onrushing Southerners with canister. The Confederates suffered about 70 casualties while the Federals lost roughly 100. On 4 December, Kilpatrick clashed again with Wheeler at Waynesboro, Georgia. Supported by Brig. Gen. Absalom Baird's XIV Corps division, the Federal horsemen drove the rebels from a series of rail barricades until they reached the streets of Waynesboro. To buy time for the withdrawal of the Confederate main body across Brier Creek to the north, Wheeler ordered Col. Thomas H. Harrison's brigade to charge the Federals. The Northerners repulsed the charge and launched a counterattack, driving the enemy cavalrymen beyond the town. Kilpatrick then burned the railroad and wagon bridges across Brier Creek to prevent Wheeler from attacking XIV Corps' rear. Confederate losses in the Battle of Waynesboro were 250 compared to the Federals' 190.

In the meantime, Sherman joined Blair's XVII Corps of the Right Wing, which had crossed the Oconee River on 26 November and the Ogeechee River four days later. On 2 December, the XVII Corps entered Millen, and word soon spread of the horrendous conditions at Camp Lawton and a mass grave that allegedly contained 650 Union dead. In reprisal, Sherman ordered Blair to burn several Confederate warehouses, the railroad depot, and a hotel. On the morning of 3 December, XIV Corps troops destroyed several miles of track on the Augusta and Savannah Railroad near Thomas' Station, five miles south of Waynesboro.

On 4 December, the two wings of Sherman's army group began the final stage of the march to Savannah. The sandy soil of the region east of Millen yielded scant sustenance to the local residents, to say nothing of 60,000 Union soldiers and their roughly 20,000 draft animals. The Federals also had their first encounter with Confederate "torpedoes." These primitive improvised explosive devices consisted of artillery shells topped with pressure fuses and were buried in the road. When exploding torpedoes severely wounded some XVII Corps soldiers, General Blair ordered a detail of Confederate prisoners to locate and remove the mines. The men in gray protested the order, claiming that such perilous duty violated their rights as prisoners of war.

Impatient with the slow progress of his columns, Sherman—having arrived on the scene by then—turned a deaf ear to their pleas. "This was not war," he later wrote, "but murder, and it made me very angry." In any event, the prisoners performed their

Union XVII Corps crossing the Ogeechee River, by Theodore R. Davis
(Harper's Weekly)

hazardous task without mishap. Although the Union commander sent one of the prisoners across the lines to warn against the further use of torpedoes, the Federals had not seen the last of the lethal devices.

TRAGEDY AT EBENEZER CREEK

Anxious to open communications with the U.S. Navy, Sherman set a brisk pace for the rest of the march. No one felt the pressure to keep up more keenly than General Davis, whose 14,000 troops of the XIV Corps lagged behind the rest of the army group. On 9 December, they marched on the old Augusta Road. Due to its flooded condition, black laborers, who worked for the Union army as pioneers, had to corduroy nearly every foot of it. About twenty-five miles from Savannah, the column came to Ebenezer Creek, which had overrun its muddy banks. Davis' engineers repaired a damaged wagon bridge and laid a pontoon bridge across the 150-foot-wide creek. As the soldiers crossed, about 600 black refugees gathered under the ancient cypress trees and waited their turn. Throughout the march, thousands of escaped slaves—or "contrabands"—had followed the Federal columns, and Sherman came to regard them as a serious drain on the armies' resources.

With Sherman's tacit consent, Davis waited until his troops were across and then ordered his engineers to destroy the wagon bridge and take up the pontoon bridge, stranding the refugees on the opposite bank. Wheeler's cavalry had stuck close to the XIV Corps, and the contrabands knew this. Many of them panicked. Old men, women, and children plunged into the freezing waters of the creek and tried to swim across. Dozens of them drowned. Wheeler's cavalry rounded up most of the remainder and presumably returned them to their masters. It is unknown if any of the captured refugees were killed or injured. The incident at Ebenezer Creek aroused considerable controversy in the North, thanks to the efforts of XIV Corps staff officer Major Connolly, who sent a scathing letter to his congressman that soon leaked to the press. When Secretary of War Edwin M. Stanton later questioned Sherman about the incident, the commanding general justified Davis' action on the grounds of military necessity. That was as far as the official inquiry went.

THE BATTLE OF FORT MCALLISTER

On 12 December, the Federals arrived near Savannah. They found the city defended by over 12,000 Confederates and 81 cannons behind thirteen miles of earthworks. Hardee's efforts to marshal dwindling Southern resources to protect the port city had clearly paid off. Moreover, their front was protected by impassable swamps and flooded rice fields, while the Savannah River covered their right flank and the Ogeechee River their left. For the past week, Sherman's army group had subsisted on beef from the cattle herd and rice, the region's staple crop. While no Union soldiers went hungry, they soon tired of the limited fare. Needless to say, Sherman was eager to open communications with the Union fleet, which was lying offshore with supplies and mail for the troops. But first the Federals would have to capture Fort McAllister, a massive earthen fortification that guarded the Ogeechee River approach to Savannah. The fort was defended by a garrison of 230 Georgia soldiers and 24 guns under Maj. George W. Anderson.

Sherman assigned the mission to his former XV Corps division, now led by Brig. Gen. William B. Hazen. On the morning of 13 December, Hazen's three brigades—numbering roughly 4,000 men—arrived opposite the fort. From prisoners the Federals learned that numerous torpedoes were buried outside McAllister's walls. Bearing this in mind, Hazen deployed his division in open formation about 600 yards from the fort. Two and a half miles away, Sherman and Howard observed Hazen's deployment from the roof of Dr. John R. Cheves' rice mill on the opposite bank of the Ogeechee. At 1645, with daylight fading, an anxious Sherman signaled Hazen to attack, and the Federals rushed the fort amid a heavy small-arms and artillery fire. Here and there a random explosion indicated that an unfortunate Union soldier had set off a torpedo. Within fifteen minutes, Hazen's men had swarmed into the fort and subdued the defenders in fierce hand-to-hand fighting. At 1700, signalmen on the rice mill roof contacted a nearby Navy vessel: "Fort McAllister is ours." In capturing the fort, the Federals had sustained over 130 casualties, while the Confederate garrison lost about 40 killed and wounded before surrendering at bayonet point.

With his supply line now open, Sherman turned his attention to capturing Savannah. On 17 December, he demanded Hardee's surrender and was promptly refused. In the meantime, Sherman continued to encircle the city while Hardee prepared to evacuate. On the night of 20–21 December, the Confederates filed out of their trenches and headed north, crossing the mile-wide Savannah River into South Carolina on a hastily improvised patchwork of earthen causeways and pontoon bridges. By dawn Hardee's entire force was safely across. Alerted by thunderous explosions along the Savannah waterfront indicating the destruction of Confederate ships and stores, Federal skirmishers rushed forward to investigate and discovered that Hardee was gone. On the morning of 21 December, Mayor Richard D. Arnold formally surrendered the city to the Federals, and, in a telegram to Washington, Sherman presented Savannah to President Lincoln as a Christmas gift. The president wrote a gracious reply in which he admitted to having doubts at the start of the campaign: "When you were about leaving Atlanta for the Atlantic coast," Lincoln began, "I was anxious, if not fearful; but, feeling that you were the better judge, and remembering 'nothing risked, nothing gained,' I did not interfere. Now, the undertaking being a success, the honor is all yours."

The March to the Sea was over. Sherman's gamble had paid off. He now shifted his gaze northward to the Carolinas and to Richmond, Virginia, the capital of the Confederacy.

Signaling the Assault on Fort McAllister, *as Generals Howard, center, and Sherman, right, study a map, by Don Troiani*
(Historical Art Prints)

Analysis

In less than four months, Sherman had captured both Atlanta and Savannah and was poised to move on to Richmond. The fall of Atlanta probably did more to ensure Lincoln's reelection in November 1864 than any other event, and the March to the Sea eliminated Georgia as a major supplier of the Confederate Army, to say nothing of the material and psychological devastation inflicted on the civilian populace. Sherman claimed that his forces confiscated or destroyed roughly $100 million worth of civilian property. Although this figure is probably inflated, the losses nevertheless were staggering, amounting to an estimated 300 miles of railroad, 5,000 horses, 4,000 mules, 13,000 cattle, 9.5 million pounds of corn, and 10.5 million pounds of fodder. There were also countless barns, bridges, cotton gins, mills, smokehouses, and other structures destroyed along the way. In addition, the Federals captured 13 locomotives, 191 rail cars, 200 heavy guns, and 35,000 bales of cotton at Savannah.

As impressive as these results were, they could not conceal the fact that Sherman had failed to crush two beleaguered Confederate armies at the close of the Atlanta and Savannah Campaigns. In both instances, he had allowed geographical objectives to assume precedence over military objectives—namely the destruction of Hood's and Hardee's forces. Even so, Sherman's three adversaries—Johnston, Hood, and Hardee—proved unable to exploit his shortcomings as a battlefield tactician. With few exceptions, the cautious Johnston had allowed Sherman to flank him out of one position after another at minimal cost to the Federals. The aggressive Hood had launched a series of futile attacks that resulted in a disastrous attrition rate of almost two Confederate casualties to one Federal lost, while Hardee was simply overwhelmed by the enormity of his task, attempting to defend both Macon and Augusta with his meager forces before hunkering down inside his fortifications at Savannah.

While Sherman's armies converged on Savannah, Thomas' command crushed Hood's army at Nashville on 16 December. Thanks to Thomas' decisive victory in Tennessee and Sherman's two triumphant campaigns in Georgia, the Confederacy teetered on the brink of collapse. Sherman now planned to combine his forces with Grant's in Virginia to defeat Lee's army, thereby bringing the war to a victorious conclusion.

THE AUTHOR

J. Britt McCarley is a native of Atlanta, Georgia, and holds a Ph.D. in history from Temple University. After working for the National Park Service, he came to the Army Historical Program in 1988 and is now the U.S. Army Training and Doctrine Command (TRADOC) chief historian and the TRADOC Military History and Heritage Program director. He is the author of *The Atlanta Campaign: A Civil War Driving Tour of Atlanta-Area Battlefields* (1989) and "'The Great Question of the Campaign Was One of Supplies': A Reinterpretation of Sherman's Generalship During the 1864 March to Atlanta in Light of the Logistic Strategy," in *Beyond Combat: Essays in Military History in Honor of Russell F. Weigley* (2007), and a contributor to *The Whirlwind War: The United States Army in Operations DESERT SHIELD and DESERT STORM* (1995).

FURTHER READINGS

Bailey, Anne J. *War and Ruin: William T. Sherman and the Savannah Campaign.* Wilmington, Del.: Scholarly Resources, 2003.

Bull, Rice C. *Soldiering: The Civil War Diary of Rice C. Bull, 123rd New York Volunteer Infantry.* Edited by K. Jack Bauer. San Rafael, Calif.: Presidio Press, 1977.

Castel, Albert E. *Decision in the West: The Atlanta Campaign of 1864.* Lawrence: University Press of Kansas, 1992.

Cox, Jacob D. *Sherman's Battle for Atlanta.* New York: Da Capo Press, 1994.

Davis, Stephen. *Atlanta Will Fall: Sherman, Joe Johnston, and the Yankee Heavy Battalions.* Wilmington, Del.: Scholarly Resources, 2001.

______. *What the Yankees Did to Us: Sherman's Bombardment and Wrecking of Atlanta.* Macon, Ga.: Mercer University Press, 2012.

Glatthaar, Joseph T. *The March to the Sea and Beyond: Sherman's Troops in the Savannah and Carolinas Campaigns.* New York: New York University Press, 1985.

Hess, Earl J. *Kennesaw Mountain: Sherman, Johnston, and the Atlanta Campaign.* Chapel Hill: University of North Carolina Press, 2013.

Kennett, Lee B. *Marching Through Georgia: The Story of Soldiers and Civilians During Sherman's Campaign.* New York: HarperCollins, 1995.

Luvaas, Jay, and Harold W. Nelson, eds. *Guide to the Atlanta Campaign: Rocky Face Ridge to Kennesaw Mountain.* The U.S. Army War College Guides to Civil War Battles. Lawrence: University Press of Kansas, 2008.

McMurry, Richard M. *Atlanta 1864: Last Chance for the Confederacy.* Lincoln: University of Nebraska Press, 2000.

Sherman, William T. *Memoirs of General W. T. Sherman.* 2 vols. New York: Library of America, 1990.

Trudeau, Noah A. *Southern Storm: Sherman's March to the Sea.* New York: HarperCollins, 2008.

Vermilya, Daniel J. *The Battle of Kennesaw Mountain.* Charleston, S.C.: History Press, 2014.

Watkins, Samuel R. *Company Aytch: Or, a Side Show of the Big Show.* New York: Plume, 1999.

For more information on the U.S. Army in the Civil War, please read other titles in the U.S. Army Campaigns of the Civil War series published by the U.S. Army Center of Military History (www.history.army.mil).

Made in the USA
Monee, IL
07 July 2026